Office of National Marine Sanctuaries
National Oceanic and Atmospheric Administration

NATIONAL MARINE
SANCTUARIES

Gray's Reef
National Marine Sanctuary

CONDITION
REPORT 2012
Addendum

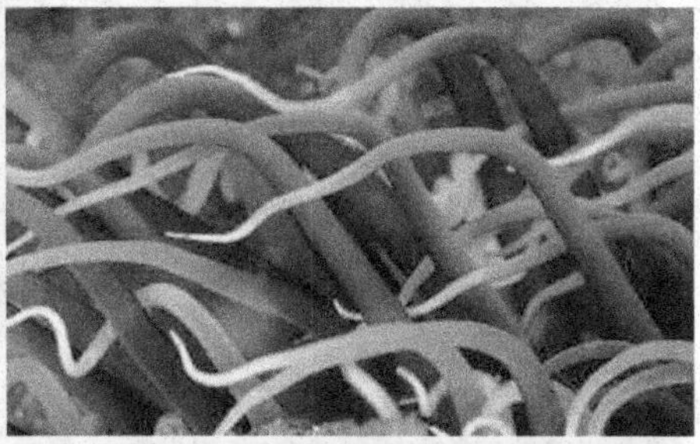

June 2012

U.S. Department of Commerce
John Bryson, Secretary

National Oceanic and Atmospheric Administration
Jane Lubchenco, Ph.D., Under Secretary of Commerce
for Oceans and Atmosphere

National Ocean Service
David M. Kennedy, Assistant Administrator

Office of National Marine Sanctuaries
Daniel J. Basta, Director

National Oceanic and Atmospheric Administration
Office of National Marine Sanctuaries
SSMC4, N/ONMS
1305 East-West Highway
Silver Spring, MD 20910
301-713-3125
http://sanctuaries.noaa.gov

Southeast Atlantic, Gulf of Mexico and Caribbean Region
NOAA Office of National Marine Sanctuaries
33 East Quay Road
Key West, Florida 33040
305-809-4670

Gray's Reef National Marine Sanctuary
10 Ocean Science Circle
Savannah, GA 31411
912-598-2345
http://graysreef.noaa.gov

Report Authors:

Gray's Reef National Marine Sanctuary:
Greg McFall, George Sedberry, Becky Shortland

Southeast Atlantic, Gulf of Mexico, and Caribbean
Region:
Sarah Fangman

Office of National Marine Sanctuaries:
Steve Gittings, Kathy Broughton

Copy Editor: Matt Dozier

Layout: Matt McIntosh

NATIONAL MARINE
SANCTUARIES

Table of Contents

About this Addendum 2

Gray's Reef National Marine Sanctuary Condition Summary Table 3

State of Sanctuary Resources 5
    Water 6
    Habitat 8
    Living Resources 11
    Maritime Archaeological Resources 17

Cited Resources 19

Additional Resources 23

Appendix A: Rating Scheme for System-Wide Monitoring Questions 24

Appendix B: Consultation with Experts and Document Review 34

Acknowledgments 36

About this Addendum

This document is an addendum to the *Gray's Reef National Marine Sanctuary 2008 Condition Report* (ONMS 2008). The 2008 report provided a summary of resources in the National Oceanic and Atmospheric Administration Gray's Reef National Marine Sanctuary (sanctuary), pressures on those resources, current conditions and trends, and management responses to the pressures that threaten the integrity of the marine environment. Specifically, the 2008 Condition Report presented responses to a set of 17 questions posed to all sanctuaries. These responses provided information on the status and trends of water quality, habitat, living resources and maritime archaeological resources, and the human activities that affect them. The 2008 report can be downloaded from the Office of National Marine Sanctuaries website at http://sanctuaries.noaa.gov/science/condition.

This addendum updates the 2008 Condition Report (ONMS 2008). The 17 questions found in the "State of Sanctuary Resources" section of the Condition Report have been reevaluated for accuracy and completeness given new data sets, published literature, and expert opinion that have become available since 2008. For those that have new information to report (questions 1, 5, 6, 8, 9, 10, 12 and 14), new status and trend ratings and updated narratives are provided. Trend ratings are generally based on observed changes in status since 2008.

In order to readdress the set of 17 questions, sanctuary staff consulted with a group of outside experts familiar with the resources and with knowledge of previous and current scientific investigations in the sanctuary. Evaluations of status and trends are based on interpretation of quantitative and, when necessary, qualitative assessments, and the observations of scientists, managers and users. The ratings reflect the collective interpretation of the status of local issues of concern among sanctuary system staff and outside experts based on their knowledge and perception of local problems. The final ratings were determined by sanctuary staff. This report has been peer reviewed and complies with the White House Office of Management and Budget's peer review standards as outlined in the Final Information Quality Bulletin for Peer Review.

This is the second effort to comprehensively describe the status and trends of resources at Gray's Reef National Marine Sanctuary. The report helps identify gaps in current monitoring efforts, as well as causal factors that may require monitoring and potential remediation in the years to come. The data discussed will not only enable resource managers and stakeholders to acknowledge prior changes in resource status, but will provide guidance for future management challenges, including the revision of the Gray's Reef National Marine Sanctuary Management Plan.

Gray's Reef National Marine Sanctuary Condition Summary Table

The following table summarizes the "State of Sanctuary Resources" section of this report. The first two columns list 17 questions used to rate the condition and trends for qualities of water, habitat, living resources, and maritime archaeological resources. The Rating column consists of a color, indicating resource condition, and a symbol, indicating trend (see key for definitions). The Basis for Judgment column provides a short statement or list of criteria used to justify the rating. The Description of Findings column presents the statement that best characterizes resource status, and corresponds to the assigned color rating. The Description of Findings statements are customized for all possible ratings for each question. Please see Appendix A for further clarification of the questions and the Description of Findings

statements. The Response column describes current or proposed management responses to pressures impacting sanctuary resources. Questions that have new information to report since the 2008 Gray's Reef National Marine Sanctuary Condition Report (ONMS 2008) are those with red numbers (questions 1, 5, 6, 8, 9, 10, 12 and 14).

Status: | Good | Good/Fair | Fair | Fair/Poor | Poor | Undet. |

Trends:
Conditions appear to be improving................................ ▲
Conditions do not appear to be changing...................... −
Conditions appear to be declining .... ▼
Undetermined trend... ?
Question not applicable... N/A

#	Questions/Resources	Rating	Basis for Judgment	Description of Findings	Sanctuary Response
WATER					
1	Are specific or multiple stressors, including changing oceanographic and atmospheric conditions, affecting water quality and how are they changing?	−	Limited data since 2000 suggest comparatively unaltered oxygen, temperature, and salinity, and some contaminants, but below EPA guidelines.	Conditions do not appear to have the potential to negatively affect living resources or habitat quality.	Recognized challenges due to coastal and inland development, population increases and climate change.
2	What is the eutrophic condition of sanctuary waters and how is it changing?	?	Comparatively unaltered levels of nutrients and chlorophyll, and lack of harmful algal blooms.	Conditions do not appear to have the potential to negatively affect living resources or habitat quality.	
3	Do sanctuary waters pose risks to human health and how are they changing?	−	2000 baseline, 2005 indicators below FDA Levels of Concern.	Selected conditions that have the potential to affect human health may exist, but human impacts have not been reported.	Continue monitoring for nutrient levels, contaminants and indicators of climate change.
4	What are the levels of human activities that may influence water quality and how are they changing?	−	Increasing human activities, but little evidence of negative effects.	Few or no activities occur that are likely to negatively affect water quality.	
HABITAT					
5	What are the abundance and distribution of major habitat types and how are they changing?	?	New map data recently collected; assessment of trends awaits comparison to earlier data.	Habitats are in pristine or near-pristine condition and are unlikely to preclude full community development.	Final management plan contains anchoring prohibition and outreach plans, and marine debris outreach, education and monitoring programs.
6	What is the condition of biologically structured habitats and how is it changing?	?	Recent data on biological assemblages suggest ephemeral nature of predominant human impacts (anchoring, fishing).	Habitats are in pristine or near-pristine condition and are unlikely to preclude full community development.	Sanctuary will enhance ongoing science to better understand biologically-structured habitat, continue monitoring benthic fauna and sediment quality, and conduct studies in research area to discern between human-induced and natural changes.
7	What are the contaminant concentrations in sanctuary habitats and how are they changing?	−	Low contaminant levels in 2000 and 2005.	Contaminants do not appear to have the potential to negatively affect living resources or water quality.	
8	What are the levels of human activities that may influence habitat quality and how are they changing?	▲	Human impacts localized within areas of heavy use.	Selected activities have resulted in measurable habitat impacts, but evidence suggests effects are localized, not widespread.	

Table is continued on the following page.

Gray's Reef National Marine Sanctuary Condition Summary Table (Continued)

#	Questions/Resources	Rating	Basis for Judgment	Description of Findings	Sanctuary Response
LIVING RESOURCES					
9	What is the status of biodiversity and how is it changing?	—	High diversity of sessile inverte-brates, benthic infaunal inverte-brate density and abundance, and algal abundance and diversity.	Biodiversity appears to reflect pristine or near-pristine conditions and pro-motes ecosystem integrity (full commu-nity development and function).	Fishing is limited to rod and reel and handline. Spearfishing is now prohib-ited. Regulations prohibit divers from taking marine organisms. A research area has been designated to evaluate impacts of bottom fishing. Education and outreach programs are in place that promote good diving techniques.

Monitoring will continue for invasive species.

Sanctuary will confirm and character-ize key species, conduct analysis of sponge mortality samples and monitor key species. |
10	What is the status of environ-mentally sustainable fishing and how is it changing?	▲	Recent data showing improve-ments in black sea bass and red snapper; need more data on non-targeted species to assess ecosystem impacts.	Extraction may inhibit full community development and function, and may cause measurable but not severe degradation of ecosystem integrity.	
11	What is the status of non-indigenous species and how is it changing?	▼	Occasional lionfish sightings in sanctuary since 2007; titan acorn barnacle, Asian green mussel and orange cup coral currently only found on manmade structures.	Non-indigenous species exist, preclud-ing full community development and function, but are unlikely to cause substantial or persistent degradation of ecosystem integrity.	
12	What is the status of key species and how is it changing?	▲	Recent improvements in black sea bass and red snapper populations.	Selected key or keystone species are at reduced levels, perhaps precluding full community development and function, but substantial or persistent declines are not expected.	
13	What is the condition or health of key species and how is it changing?	?	Key species tentatively identi-fied but condition and health undetermined; some contami-nants detected in sponges, black seabass and arc shells.	N/A	
14	What are the levels of human activities that may influence living resource quality and how are they changing?	▲	Localized within areas of heavy use, with reduced pressure in certain areas due to management actions and the status of the economy, but trend data limited, suggesting a significant monitor-ing gap.	Selected activities have resulted in measurable living resource impacts, but evidence suggests effects are localized, not widespread.	
MARITIME ARCHAEOLOGICAL RESOURCES					
15	What is the integrity of known maritime archaeological re-sources and how is it changing?	N/A	No archaeological evidence, though former human occupation remains a possibility based on paleontological data.	N/A	Anchoring has been banned, in part to reduce threat to archaeological resources.
16	Do known maritime archaeo-logical resources pose an environmental hazard and is this threat changing?	N/A	No archaeological evidence, though former human occupation remains a possibTility based on paleontological data.	N/A	
17	What are the levels of human activities that may influence maritime archaeological re-source quality and how are they changing?	—	Potential for diving and fishing to damage sites.	Some potentially relevant activities exist, but they do not appear to have had a negative effect on maritime archaeological resource integrity.	

State of Sanctuary Resources

This section provides summaries of the status and trends within four resource areas: water, habitat, living resources, and maritime archaeological resources. For each, sanctuary staff and selected outside experts considered a series of questions about each resource area. The set of questions is derived from the Office of National Marine Sanctuaries' mission and a system-wide monitoring framework (NMSP 2004) developed to ensure the timely flow of data and information to those responsible for managing and protecting resources in the ocean and coastal zone, and to those that use, depend on, and study the ecosystems encompassed by the sanctuaries. The questions address information needs that are common to nearly all sanctuaries throughout the sanctuary system. Appendix A (Rating Scheme for System-Wide Monitoring Questions) clarifies the set of questions and presents statements that were used to judge the status and assign a corresponding color code on a scale from "good" to "poor." These statements are customized for each question. In addition, the following options are available for all questions: "N/A" – the question does not apply; and "undetermined" – resource status is undetermined. In addition, symbols are used to indicate trends: " ▲ " – conditions appear to be improving; "—" – conditions do not appear to be changing; " ▼ " – conditions appear to be declining; and "?" – the trend is undetermined.

Based on an evaluation of new data, published literature, and expert opinion that have become available since the publication of the 2008 report (ONMS 2008), new ratings and narratives were developed for eight of the 17 questions (1, 5, 6, 8, 9, 10, 12, and 14). Ratings are supported by specific examples of data, investigations, monitoring and observations, and the basis for judgment is provided in the text and summarized in the table for each resource area. Where published or additional information exists, the reader is provided with appropriate references and Web links.

Ratings for a number of questions depend on judgments involving "ecological integrity," and an ecosystem's status with regard to it. This is because one of the foundational principles behind the establishment of marine sanctuaries is to protect ocean ecosystems. But this concept can be confusing, and is interpreted in different ways, so it is important to provide clarification of its application within this report. Ecological integrity implies the presence of naturally occurring species, populations and communities, and ecological processes functioning at appropriate rates, scales, and levels of natural variation, as well as the environmental conditions that support these attributes (modified from National Park Service Vital Signs monitoring program: http://science.nature.nps.gov/im/monitor/Glossary.cfm). Ecosystems have integrity when they have their native components intact, including abiotic components (the physical elements, such as water and habitats), biodiversity (the composition and abundance of species and communities in an ecosystem), and ecosystem processes (the engines that makes ecosystem work (e.g., space competition, predation, symbioses) (from Parks Canada at http://www.pc.gc.ca/progs/np-pn/ie-ei.aspx). For purposes of this report, the level of integrity that is judged to exist is based on the extent to which humans have altered key attributes, and the effect of that change on the ability of an ecosystem to resist continued change and recover from it. The statements for many questions are intended to reflect this judgment. Reference is made in the rating system to "near-pristine" conditions, which for this report would imply a status as near to an unaltered ecosystem as we can reasonably presume to exist, recognizing that there are virtually no ecosystems on Earth completely free from human influence.

Not all questions, however, use ecological integrity as a basis for judgment. One focuses on the impacts of water quality factors on human health. Another rates the status of key species compared with that expected in an unaltered ecosystem. One rates maritime archaeological resources based on their historical, archaeological, scientific and educational value. Another considers the level and persistence of localized threats posed by degrading archaeological resources. Finally, four ask specifically about the levels of ongoing human activity that could affect resource condition.

Water

Contaminants may be transported from land across the inner shelf to Gray's Reef National Marine Sanctuary, but the quantity of material from this process is affected by the trapping efficiency of salt marsh estuaries. The concentration of nutrients in the water not only varies with outwelling intensity, which is affected by freshwater input and oceanographic events, but also with the rates of exchange of contaminants between the water and silt-clay particles in the sediments.

NOAA's National Ocean Service has conducted sampling along three cross-shelf transects, extending from the mouths of Sapelo, Doboy and Altamaha sounds, and showed a general pattern of decreasing concentrations of contaminants with increasing distance from shore, suggesting sources from discharge through coastal sounds. Data also revealed higher percentages of silt-clay fractions in sediments at stations closest to the sounds. These finer-grained particles represent a potential source of adsorbed chemical contaminants discharged from these systems. Cross-shelf differences in salinity and temperature provided additional evidence of the influence of the sounds, especially the Altamaha, on the adjacent shelf environment. The atmosphere is also considered a pathway of contaminants such as heavy metals, persistent organic contaminants and nutrients to the reef (NMSP 2006). In addition, there is potential for Gulf Stream intrusions to carry contaminants from further south.

The following information provides an assessment, made by sanctuary staff and subject matter experts, of the status and trends pertaining to the current state of water quality in Gray's Reef National Marine Sanctuary.

1. *Are specific or multiple stressors, including changing oceanographic and atmospheric conditions, affecting water quality?*

Based on limited assessments conducted since 2000, water quality in the sanctuary is considered to be "good." Conditions do not appear to be changing. The revised ratings since the 2008 report reflect information gathered in recent years through water monitoring and process studies (Question 1 received a status and trend rating of "undetermined" in the 2008 Condition Report).

Specific chemical contaminants have not been measured in the water column but are expected to be very low or undetectable because of the low concentrations found in sediments and biota. In addition, a bacterial indicator of chemical contamination (ratio of bioluminescence to total bacteria; Frischer et al. 2005) suggests an absence of chemical contaminants in the water column at the Gray's Reef sanctuary (Frischer unpubl. data). Dissolved oxygen levels, a primary indicator of water quality, are high throughout the sanctuary. Results of a baseline characterization conducted in 2000 (Cooksey et al. 2004, Hyland et al. 2006) in-dicated that dissolved oxygen values ranged from 7.6-8.4 mg l^{-1}, which are well above a reported benthic hypoxic effect threshold of about 1.4 mg l^{-1} (Diaz and Rosenberg 1995) and most state standards of 5 mg l^{-1} or lower. A follow-up survey conducted in 2005 and ongoing monitoring showed consistent values in this same range (Balthis et al. 2007, Frischer unpubl. data).

In 2005-07, sanctuary staff collaborated with the Skidaway Institute of Oceanography to improve water quality monitoring. The purpose was to assess whether trends observed in the coastal region are reflected in water quality at Gray's Reef. Measurements of temperature, salinity and dissolved oxygen (and other productivity-related measures discussed in Question 2) suggest that water quality conditions are comparatively unaltered and are unlikely to negatively affect sanctuary resources. And while there is some concern that large-scale changes in oceanographic and atmospheric conditions (e.g., factors related to climate change, such as storm frequency and acidification) may affect water quality, there is insufficient information to determine whether changes have occurred yet.

Currently, anthropogenic stressors that may affect the water quality in the sanctuary — including increasing human activity in the coastal zone — are relatively low. Although some contaminants have been identified in fish and benthic organisms, to date, all have been below FDA guidelines. However, potential problems do exist. As coastal development and population density continues to increase, offshore water quality may be impacted. This possibility was suggested by a recent study investigating the connectivity between the Altamaha River and the sanctuary (Cohen and Gleason unpubl. data). In this study, 190 liters of a nontoxic, fluorescent dye (Rhodamine WT) were released in the Altamaha River Sound in south Georgia on an outgoing tide. Three days later, this dye was detected within the boundaries of the sanctuary, suggesting that the Altamaha and other rivers along the Georgia coast can be sources of both nutrients and contaminants for habitats and organisms in the sanctuary.

Changing salinity patterns on the continental shelf off Georgia are also potential agents of change for coastal and shelf species that inhabit Gray's Reef. Natural drought (currently ranging from severe to exceptional in most of Georgia) and increasing human freshwater extraction from dwindling watersheds have had dramatic effects on coastal ecosystems recently (Visser et al. 2002). Freshwater runoff is known to reach the Gulf Stream, and is particularly strong during winter and early spring (Li 2001) when many reef fish spawn (Sedberry et al. 2006). The runoff typically carries nutrients from terrestrial sources to ocean waters (Atkinson et al. 1978) that are habitat for fish larvae; reduced runoff could result in poor survival of reef fish larvae on the shelf.

In addition, the levels of freshwater runoff can affect shelf circulation, and their penetration across the shelf can affect Gulf Stream meanders (Atkinson et al. 1978, Blanton 1981) that influence the kinds of organisms found at Gray's Reef. Because Gray's Reef is located within the influence of a massive estuarine/riverine system, it typically has salinities lower than the open ocean, and species typical of coastal and estuarine habitats can be found there. Reduced freshwater runoff could influence the fauna of Gray's Reef, as oceanic and Gulf Stream species replace coastal species that are less tolerant of higher salinities. Enhanced monitoring of these coastal and offshore influences will be essential to staging effective responses by sanctuary and coastal resource managers in the event of unnatural change.

2. *What is the eutrophic condition of sanctuary waters and how is it changing?*

At present, eutrophication does not appear to have the potential to negatively affect living resources or habitat quality; therefore, this question is rated as "good." Insufficient data exist, however, to determine whether temporal trends have occurred.

Productivity-related measurements in 2005-07 in cooperation with the Skidaway Institute of Oceanography include dissolved oxygen, inorganic nutrients (NO_2/NO_3, NH_4, PO_4, $Si(OH)_4$), organic nutrients (DON, urea, DOC), chlorophyll-a, and a number of bacteriological parameters, including total bacteria counts, total and fecal coliforms, enterococci, and the ratio of bioluminescent to total heterotrophic bacteria. There is no evidence of eutrophication or incipient eutrophication at Gray's Reef National Marine Sanctuary, as is occurring in the South Atlantic Bight coastal zone (Verity et al. 2006). This finding is based on low and stable nutrient concentrations, seasonal estimates of chlorophyll-a concentrations, the absence of harmful algal bloom events — with the exception of a subsurface bloom of *Phaeocystis globosa* in 1999 associated with stratified water (Long et al. 2007) — and high and stable dissolved oxygen concentrations in surface and near-bottom waters. The cause of this bloom was not identified and has not occurred again. In addition, eutrophication is not likely to become an issue due to the well-mixed nature of the coastal estuaries and shelf of the South Atlantic Bight and the fact that there is minimal variability in the rates of change of nutrient loads and oxygen in adjacent coastal waters (Verity et al. 2006).

3. *Do sanctuary waters pose risks to human health?*

While conditions that have the potential to affect human health may exist at Gray's Reef, human impacts have not been reported; therefore, this question is rated as "good/fair." Furthermore, there is no evidence that the threat is changing. Risks to human health in the Gray's Reef sanctuary have been undergoing assessment based on bacterial indicators of fecal contamination. Indicators have included total and fecal coliform bacteria and enterococci bacteria. All indicators were below detection limits in eight samples collected throughout 2005 (Frischer unpubl. data), suggesting minimal risks to human health.

Results of a baseline characterization of benthic communities and sediment quality conducted in 2000 (Cooksey et al. 2004, Hyland et al. 2006) suggested that chemical contaminants in tissues of target benthic species within the sanctuary were below FDA human health guidelines (where available), based on a limited sample population of fillets from 10 black sea bass (*Centropristis striata*) and nine arc shell (*Arca zebra*) composites. Moderate concentrations of lead, just below the FDA Level of Concern value of 3 µg/g dry weight, were found in one fish sample (2.6 µg/g) and one arc shell sample (2.9 µg/g). Also, similar to sediments (see Question 7), tissues of both species contained trace concentrations of man-made pesticides (DDT, chlorpyrifos, dieldrin, lindane, heptachlor epoxide) and other chemical substances associated with human sources (PCBs, PAHs). The fact that immobile organisms like the arcs picked up these contaminants, albeit at low concentrations, provides evidence that such materials have made their way to the offshore sanctuary environment, either by air or cross-shelf transport by water from land, or as a result of boat use in the sanctuary. Results of a follow-up monitoring survey conducted in 2005 (Balthis et al. 2007) show a similar persistent trend of low yet detectable levels of chemical contaminants in tissues of these same species. Also, migratory species of fish like king mackerel (*Scomberomorus cavalla*) that are currently under contaminant warnings (e.g., for mercury) are actively fished within sanctuary waters.

4. *What are the levels of human activities that may influence water quality and how are they changing?*

Because of the remote location[1] of Gray's Reef National Marine Sanctuary from the coastal zone, few or no activities occur that are likely to negatively affect water quality; therefore, this question

---

[1] Gray's Reef National Marine Sanctuary is one of the largest nearshore live-bottom reefs in the southeastern United States, and it is the only marine protected area in federal waters (U.S. Exclusive Economic Zone) in the South Atlantic Bight, an area of the continental shelf stretching from Cape Hatteras, N.C., to Cape Canaveral, Fla. Located 17.5 nautical miles offshore of Sapelo Island, Ga., the 16.68-square-nautical-mile sanctuary contains both rocky ledges and sandy flats. Unlike reefs built by corals, Gray's Reef comprises scattered limestone rock outcroppings that stand above the sandy substrate of the nearly flat continental shelf. The reef also supports soft corals, non-reef-building hard corals, bivalves and sponges, as well as associated fishes and sea turtles. For more information, see the "Site History" section of the 2008 Gray's Reef National Marine Sanctuary Condition Report (ONMS 2008).

is rated "good." Human activities have increased dramatically along the southeastern coastal zone, but based on chemical contaminant and nutrient concentrations measured in the sanctuary there is no evidence of impact from these sources and no evidence that the trends observed in the coastal zone during the past 20 years (Verity et al. 2006) are mirrored in the sanctuary. However, the continued development of the coastal zone is inevitable, and therefore, continued monitoring of the Gray's Reef sanctuary for evidence of this impact should be a continuing research priority. Furthermore, the recent confirmation of connectivity between river outflow and surface waters over hard-bottom reefs of the Georgia coast (Cohen and Gleason unpubl. data) links the health of the sanctuary to development and other activities that occur farther inland.

Water Quality Status & Trends

#	Issue	Rating	Basis for Judgment	Description of Findings
1	Stressors	—	Limited data since 2000 suggest comparatively unaltered oxygen, temperature, and salinity, and some contaminants, but below EPA guidelines.	Conditions do not appear to have the potential to negatively affect living resources or habitat quality.
2	Eutrophic Condition	?	Comparatively unaltered levels of nutrients and chlorophyll, and lack of harmful algal blooms.	Conditions do not appear to have the potential to negatively affect living resources or habitat quality.
3	Human Health	—	2000 baseline, 2005 indicators below FDA Levels of Concern.	Selected conditions that have the potential to affect human health may exist, but human impacts have not been reported
4	Human Activities	—	Increasing human activities, but little evidence of negative effects.	Few or no activities occur that are likely to negatively affect water quality.

Status: Good   Good/Fair   Fair   Fair/Poor   Poor   Undet.

Trends: Improving (▲), Not Changing (—), Declining (▼). Undetermined Trend (**?**), Question not applicable (**N/A**)

Habitat

Gray's Reef is a submerged hard-bottom (calcitic sandstone) area that, compared to surrounding areas, contains extensive but discontinuous rock outcroppings of moderate (1-2 meters/4-6 feet) height with sandy, flat-bottomed troughs between. The series of rock ledges and sand expanses has produced a complex habitat of caves, burrows, troughs and overhangs that provide a solid base upon which the sanctuary's abundant sessile invertebrates attach and grow. This rocky platform, with its carpet of attached organisms, is known as a "live-bottom habitat." This topography supports an unusual assemblage of temperate and tropical marine flora and fauna. Algae and invertebrates grow on the exposed rock surfaces; dominant invertebrates include sponges, barnacles, sea fans, hard corals, sea stars, crabs, lobsters, snails and shrimp. The reef attracts numerous species of benthic and pelagic fishes, including black sea bass, red snapper, grouper and mackerel.

The following information provides an assessment, made by sanctuary staff and subject matter experts, of the status and trends pertaining to the current state of habitat in Gray's Reef National Marine Sanctuary.

5. What are the abundance and distribution of major habitat types and how are they changing?

To assess the abundance and distribution of major habitat types in Gray's Reef, the sanctuary completed the first comprehensive habitat classification in 2001 using multibeam and side-scan sonar surveys, ground-truthed by diver observations and ROV video and still photography (Kendall et al. 2005). The sonar imagery, which completely covers the sanctuary, was used to create a mosaic and georeferenced for use in GIS analysis of bottom type and benthic habitats. This analysis documents the four major habitat types and their spatial extent in the sanctuary: densely colonized live bottom (0.6%), sparsely colonized live bottom (24.8%), rippled sand (66.9%) and flat sand (7.7%) (Figure 1). Because of recent management efforts (e.g., prohibiting anchoring in the sanctuary and establishing a Research Area), and a lack of information suggesting alterations, the status of the abundance and distribution of major habitat types now is considered to be "good." (Question 5 received a status rating of "good/fair" and a trend rating of "undetermined" in the 2008 Condition Report).

A recent survey of 179 sites within the Gray's Reef sanctuary indicates that the four bottom types have distinct physical and biological characteristics (Kendall et al. 2007). Sparse live bottom and ledges are colonized by macroalgae and numerous invertebrates, including coral, gorgonians, sponges, tunicates, anemones and bryozoans. Biotic cover on sparse live bottom is less in comparison to ledges, likely because colonization is inhibited by shifting sands. In addition, percent cover of biota on ledges is positively related to ledge height (Kendall et al. 2007). The densely colonized live bottom, although comprising a small percentage of the total sanctuary area, is the critical habitat impacted by pressures and is disproportionate in its importance. Thus, small impacts to a very spatially limited habitat are a particular management concern for the sanctuary. Anthropogenic

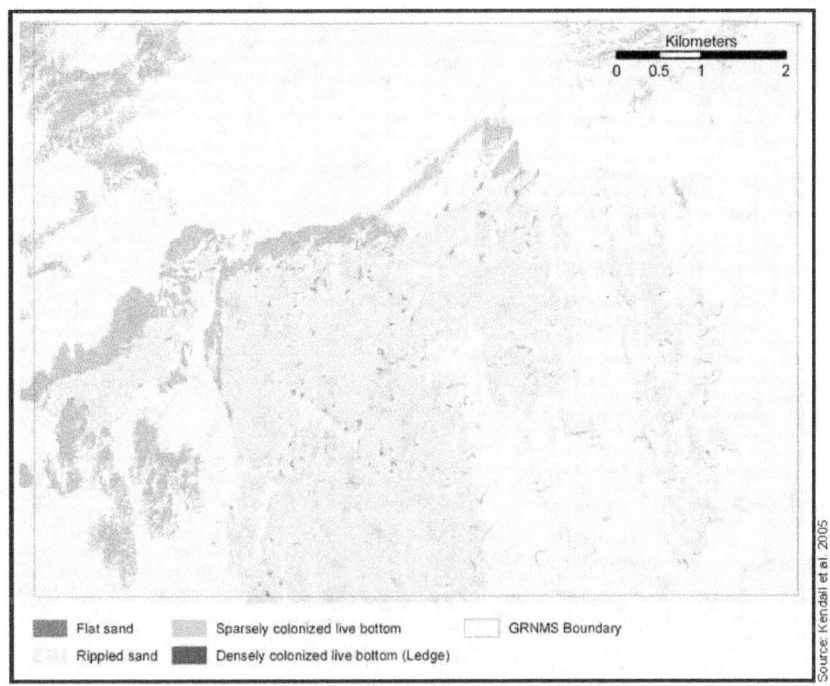

Source: Kendall et al. 2005

Flat sand   Sparsely colonized live bottom   GRNMS Boundary
Rippled sand   Densely colonized live bottom (Ledge)

Figure 1. Gray's Reef National Marine Sanctuary benthic habitat map.

pressures are not significantly affecting the abundance or distribution of habitat types based on diver observations. Although flat and rippled sand bottom have a low percent cover of epibenthic organisms, these bottom types harbor diverse infaunal assemblages (Hyland et al. 2006).

Previous side-scan surveys of the sanctuary in the 1980s were used to characterize bottom types. Direct comparisons with the new, multibeam datasets are not straightforward because of differences in available data types and line spacing. However, efforts to quantify the level of error in older data are ongoing so that decadal changes in habitat distribution can potentially be determined. Preliminary comparisons suggest that some areas of low relief in the southeastern quadrant of the sanctuary have been buried by influx of sand on these timescales. New multibeam data were collected for the entire sanctuary in 2011; however, these data have not been fully analyzed, and therefore, changes to the abundance and distribution of major habitat types have not been determined. The establishment of a Research Area on Dec. 4, 2011, within the sanctuary was intended, in part, to allow for investigations into the effects of human activities and natural processes on habitats and natural resources.

6. *What is the condition of biologically structured habitats and how is it changing?*

The condition of biologically structured habitat is considered to be "good," as evidenced by benthic invertebrate and algae data, as well as diver observation (Wagner 2006; Freeman et al. 2007; Greene 2008; Ruzicka and Gleason 2008, 2009; Sanamyan et al. 2009). There is, however, evidence of anchor, fishing and storm damage in addition to naturally occurring seasonal changes (including storm and hurricane events) in the biotic structure of the reefs. The trend is "undetermined." The change in the status rating from the 2008 report is due to considerable new information on the abundance and distribution of biological assemblages on the different bottom types present in the sanctuary (Question 6 received a status and trend rating of "undetermined" in the 2008 Condition Report).

Gray's Reef National Marine Sanctuary is composed of four main bottom types: flat sand, rippled sand, sparsely colonized live bottom and densely colonized live bottom (ledges). Non-quantitative assessments and observations (e.g., dislodgement of sponges, corals and other invertebrates) by scientists and sanctuary staff indicates that damage to densely and sparsely colonized live bottom (which was primarily associated with anchoring), has now been greatly reduced due to the prohibition on anchoring. Recreational fishing may also impact biologically structured habitats through marine debris, especially through entanglement in monofilament line (Kendall et al. 2007). Although the impact is minimal, disturbances by divers are also occurring. Damage to biologically structured habitats is disproportionate on a spatial scale and is probably concentrated in areas of highest fishing and diving activity. Recently established long-term monitoring of the benthos indicates that changes in biologically structured benthic habitats also occur due to storm impacts (i.e., movement of sediment) or on seasonal cycles (Gleason et al. in prep). The inability to decipher changes resulting from human impacts versus natural processes makes the trend undetermined at present. Continued monitoring at a range of spatial and temporal scales is required to establish the trend.

7. What are the contaminant concentrations in sanctuary habitats and how are they changing?

Contaminant concentrations in sanctuary habitats do not appear to have the potential to negatively affect living resources or water quality; therefore, this question is rated as "good." Conditions do not appear to be changing. Results of a baseline characterization of benthic communities and sediment quality conducted in 2000 (Hyland et al. 2006, Cooksey et al. 2004) suggested that chemical contaminants in sediments (including pesticides, PCBs, PAHs and metals) were generally at low background concentrations, below probable bioeffect threshold levels. An additional contaminant study in Gray's Reef planned for summer 2012 will provide further information on contaminant levels in the sanctuary, and which levels can be compared to the previous studies to evaluate trends.

The historically low sediment contamination is most likely attributable to the remote location of this offshore environment and the sandy nature of the substrate (e.g., absence of a silt-clay fraction). Studies by the Environmental Protection Agency and NOAA (Cooksey et al. 2010) have shown that contaminants are generally low throughout the entire South Atlantic Bight. However, sediments contain trace concentrations of contaminants associated with human sources (pesticides, PCBs, PAHs), demonstrating that such materials are making their way to the offshore sanctuary environment, either by air or aquatic cross-shelf transport from land (Figure 2). Total organic carbon in sediments is also at low levels — less than 2 percent throughout the sanctuary and less than 1 percent at most stations (Hyland et al. 2006) — typical of shelf waters in this region (Tenore et al. 1978). This is well below a reported range (less than 3.6 percent) associated with a high risk of disturbance from organic over-enrichment (Hyland et al. 2005). Results of a follow-up monitoring survey conducted in 2005 (Balthis et al. 2007) showed a similar persistent trend of low background levels of such

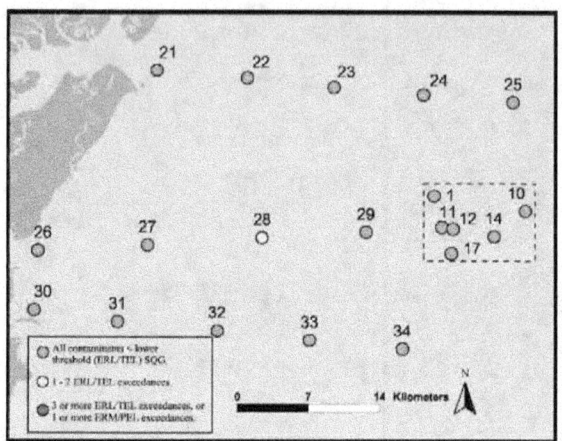

Figure 2. Spring 2001 summary of chemical contaminant concentrations in sediments relative to sediment quality guidelines. The outlined box to the right of the image indicates the Gray's Reef National Marine Sanctuary boundary.

sediment-associated stressors. Nonetheless, the presence of chemical contaminants in sediments at low yet detectable levels in both surveys suggests that such pollutants have reached the sanctuary (NMSP 2006). This result, combined with 1) a wealth of data showing that urbanized watersheds deliver pollutants such as pesticides (Hunt et al. 1999), mercury (Thompson et al. 2000), PAHs (Walker et al. 2004) and excess nitrogen (McClelland et al. 1997, Fry et al. 2003, Cohen and Fong 2006) from human sources to the coast and 2) demonstrated connectivity between Georgia river outflows and the sanctuary (Cohen and Gleason unpubl. data), suggest that monitoring for contaminants should continue in order to ensure that future problems do not develop and to explore other potential sources of contaminants (e.g., atmospheric deposition).

8. What are the levels of human activities that may influence habitat quality and how are they changing?

Selected human activities in the sanctuary have resulted in measurable habitat impacts, but evidence suggests the effects are localized and not widespread; therefore, this question is rated as "fair." The trend is "improving," in part due to new regulatory actions that have been implemented, including a ban on anchoring (2006), a spearfishing ban (2010) and the establishment of a Research Area (2011) (Question 8 received a status rating of "fair" and a trend rating of "undetermined" in the 2008 Condition Report). Fishing, anchoring, marine debris, divers and research activities are suspected or known causes of damage to habitats within Gray's Reef National Marine Sanctuary (Bauer et al. 2008, 2010). Based on boat counts and fishing tournament participation data, visitation to Gray's Reef has increased over the last 25 years, and this increase is likely responsible for some documented habitat impacts. Anchor damage and entangled fishing line has been observed, although the occurrence of these appears to be decreasing since the anchoring ban implemented in 2006 (McFall, GRNMS, pers. comm.). The spatial distribution of debris is concentrated in the center of the sanctuary and is most frequently associated with biologically structured habitats (i.e., habitats created by sponges and other organisms with erect body forms) and along ledges, rather than at other bottom types. Approximately 90% of debris encountered at the Gray's Reef sanctuary has been found along ledges (Kendall et al. 2007). Data are not currently available to discern any changes in the number of visitors participating in destructive activities, but in light of the current economy, fuel prices, and fisheries management regulations, visitation is presumed to be lower. Nevertheless, continued increases in human use will probably add to habitat alteration. A combination of improved monitoring and enhanced education and enforcement of regulations would be appropriate management actions to mitigate potential damage due to increased public use. Additional human activities that occur outside the boundaries of the sanctuary (e.g., climate change, vessel traffic, invasive species) may influence habitat quality inside the sanctuary; however, information on the levels and effects of those activities are not yet known.

Habitat Status & Trends

#	Issue	Rating	Basis for Judgment	Description of Findings
5	Abundance/ Distribution	?	New map data recently collected; assessment of trends awaits comparison to earlier data.	Habitats are in pristine or near-pristine condition and are unlikely to preclude full community development.
6	Structure	?	Recent data on biological assemblages suggest ephemeral nature of predominant human impacts (anchoring, fishing).	Habitats are in pristine or near-pristine condition and are unlikely to preclude full community development.
7	Contaminants	—	Low contaminant levels in 2000 and 2005.	Contaminants do not appear to have the potential to negatively affect living resources or water quality.
8	Human Impacts	▲	Human impacts localized within areas of heavy use.	Selected activities have resulted in measurable habitat impacts, but evidence suggests effects are localized, not widespread.

Status: Good Good/Fair Fair Fair/Poor Poor Undet.

Trends: Improving (▲), Not Changing (—), Getting Worse (▼), Undetermined Trend (?), Question not applicable (N/A)

Living Resources

The live-bottom reefs of the sanctuary are composed of high assemblages of invertebrate endofaunal organisms and a high diversity and abundance of benthic infaunal invertebrates — an important food source for forage fishes and some fishery species. The highest fish species richness, diversity, abundance and biomass at Gray's Reef National Marine Sanctuary are found on and near reef structure ('live bottom') (Kendall et al. 2009). Resident and non-resident reef fishes normally associate with hard structures, and even coastal pelagic species such as mackerel are attracted to and orient themselves near structures. Flat and rippled sand sites have the lowest fish species richness, diversity, abundance and biomass. Analysis of fish assemblages at ledges (high-relief hard structure areas) indicates that species richness and total abundance of fish are positively related to total percent cover of sessile invertebrates and ledge height (Kendall et al. 2007, Kendall et al. 2008, Kendall et al. 2009). As a result, ledges within the sanctuary are often targeted by fishermen. In addition, migratory pelagic species like king mackerel and amberjack feed on baitfish (small pelagic schooling fishes) and epibenthic resident reef fish species that concentrate near exposed hard bottom and vertical relief on the seafloor.

The following information provides an assessment, made by sanctuary staff and subject matter experts, of the status and trends pertaining to the current state of living resources in Gray's Reef National Marine Sanctuary.

9. What is the status of biodiversity and how is it changing?

The status of biodiversity in the Gray's Reef sanctuary is considered to be "good" based on the high diversity of sessile invertebrates, benthic infaunal invertebrate density and abundance, and algal abundance and diversity in the sanctuary. Data on the fish community may suggest a slightly lower status rating due to the effects of fishing pressure (discussed further in question 10); overall, however, the biodiversity within Gray's Reef is rated as good. Because abundance and diversity of benthic sessile and infaunal invertebrates have consistently been high, the trend is not changing. The changes in ratings since the 2008 report reflect additional data in recent years from more taxa (Question 9 received a status and trend rating of "undetermined" in the 2008 Condition Report).

Benthic infaunal invertebrate diversity in the Gray's Reef sanctuary is high (invertebrates that live within the bottom substrate). Species richness of benthic infauna was consistently high between the year 2000 (mean number of taxa per sample = 44, total number of species from 20 stations = 348) and a follow-up study in 2005 (mean number of taxa per sample = 47, total number of species from 20 stations = 353) (Hyland et al. 2006, Balthis et al. 2007). The two studies produced a combined total of 483 taxa. Benthic infauna are an important food source for forage fishes and some fishery species and are an important link in the food chain (Posey et al. 2002).

A study was conducted at Gray's Reef to characterize the assemblages of invertebrate organisms which live on or in a living host (endofauna). Twenty-four epifaunal hosts were found to contain a total of 132,056 solitary and 61 colonial associates belonging to 115 taxonomic groups, demonstrating that epifaunal sponges and octocorals in the sanctuary provide important habitat for abundant and diverse assemblages of associated endofauna (Greene 2008).

The diversity of sessile invertebrates on hard substrata is currently high. For example, 52 species of sponges have been identified from hard-bottom reefs in and around the sanctuary, two of which are thought to be un-described species and 15 of which are new records for the area (Freeman et al. 2007). The sanctuary is located at the convergence of temperate and tropical water masses and, as such, the sponges found in the sanctuary are representative of both regions. Other groups of sessile invertebrates, including cnidarians, bryozoans and tunicates, are also common. Benthic surveys conducted at 37 different reef sites within the sanctuary in summer 2011 found a mean sessile invertebrate species diversity of approximately 12 species per square meter and a mean percent cover of 66% (Gleason et al. in prep.).

Studies conducted since 2004 at a hard-bottom site outside the sanctuary but within the general region suggest that the composition of the benthic invertebrate community can vary both seasonally and annually (Gleason, pers. comm.). Even with this variability, the percent cover and species diversity in continually revisited 30x30 centimeter control plots has remained stable from 2004 to the present. In contrast, 30x30 centimeter plots cleared of all benthic organisms in 2004 have been slow to recover. Species diversity and percent cover have steadily increased in cleared plots, but even six years after the initial manipulation both of these parameters are significantly lower than those observed in control plots. These results suggest that while the current condition of the sessile benthic community appears to be good within the sanctuary and community development proceeds slowly as a normal condition, recovery time from any substantial mortality event could be substantial.

Benthic surveys were conducted by Goldberg and Heine in June and July 2011 to describe algal diversity in the northern and southern areas of the sanctuary and to compare the data to studies conducted previously by Searles (1987). During these surveys, 55 algal species were recorded, eight of which were not reported in the study conducted by Searles (Goldberg unpubl. data).

Fish diversity is also quite high in the sanctuary, with about 200 species recorded, including 46 managed species (Hare et al. unpubl. MS, GRNMS unpubl. data). Annual monitoring has indicated no significant change in fish diversity in visual census-

es from 2003 to 2011 (REEF unpubl. data) or in fish trap catches from 1993 to 2002 (Barkoukis 2006). Shannon's diversity index for fish diversity estimates measured from the 2011 benthic surveys ranged from 0.53 – 2.29, and averaged 1.66 (± 0.06) (Muñoz and Whitfield, in prep). The Gray's Reef sanctuary is in a transitional zone between cold temperate and warm temperate waters. Factors such as seasonal and episodic hydrographic events, cold water intrusions, wave activity, sand movement, ledge dynamics and Gulf Stream eddies, undoubtedly contribute to the high diversity observed in the sanctuary.

Recent studies of facilitative interactions between pelagic and demersal piscivores at the Gray's Reef sanctuary demonstrate that behavioral interactions related to prey capture are common attributes of these fish communities (Auster et al. 2009, 2012, in review). In this case, pelagic piscivores attack and drive prey towards reefs where predator avoidance responses produce ephemeral feeding opportunities for demersal piscivores. Sixty-seven percent of 274 predation events observed between 2009 and 2011 involved interactions between mid-water and demersal predators. Such interactions enhance feeding rates for demersal piscivores and may yield benefits for growth and reproduction due to energetic subsidies. Based on functional group roles, large-size-class demersal piscivores can replace pelagic piscivores in the mid-water above reefs when the latter group is absent. If fishing pressure removes pelagic piscivores from local reefs, then large sizes of demersal species can provide a functional redundancy in the community and can fill this role. However, such interactions would be sensitive to overfishing. Interaction strengths between species and functional groups can be quantified based on data collected by diver surveys, and this approach can produce useful measures of variation in behavior webs over time and between areas open and closed to fishing.

10. *What is the status of environmentally sustainable fishing and how is it changing?*

According to NOAA's National Marine Fisheries Service (2012, http://www.nmfs.noaa.gov/sfa/statusoffisheries/SOSmain.htm), species that are sought by anglers at Gray's Reef and that are overfished include red grouper (*Epinephelus morio*) and red snapper (*Lutjanus campechanus*). Black sea bass, gag, red grouper and red snapper are undergoing overfishing. Red snapper, gag, and black sea bass have strong interactions as co-occurring predators in behavior webs. Overfishing could potentially result in indirect effects on feeding rates of predators with related effects on growth rates and reproduction (Auster et al. in review).

Despite several species being considered overfished or undergoing overfishing, the status of environmentally sustainable fishing is considered "fair." The trend is "improving" based on evidence of increasing numbers and sizes of black sea bass in Marine Resources Monitoring, Assessment and Prediction (MARMAP) surveys and the additional establishment of fisheries regulations by SAFMC since the 2008 Condition Report (Question 10 received a status rating of "fair/poor" and a trend rating of "declining" in the 2008 Condition Report). The complete closure of the fishery for red snapper is resulting in rebuilding of the stock, and a rebuilding plan will be implemented for red grouper in June 2012.

Currently, recreational fishing pressure on reef-associated fishes is thought to be less intense than it is for pelagic species, although studies conducted at the Gray's Reef sanctuary indicate that fishing mortality for black sea bass has been the same or higher within the sanctuary than it is regionally or at inner-shelf reefs off South Carolina (Harris et al. 2005). The most intensive fishing pressure occurs in conjunction with offshore fishing tournaments, which target king mackerel (*Scomberomorus cavalla*). More fishing activity occurs on weekends than during weekdays. On an annual basis, fishing pressure is patterned around meteorological events and migratory patterns of the targeted species. Fishing pressure is probably lowest in mid-winter with low temperatures and winter storms. By late winter or early spring, recreational fishing pressure increases as the anglers target black sea bass. In late spring to early summer, fishing pressure peaks as anglers target the pelagic cobia (*Rachycentron canadum*), bluefish (*Pomatomus saltatrix*), Spanish mackerel (*S. maculates*) and king mackerel. Late summer experiences a slump in fishing pressure as target species are widely scattered and difficult to catch. By fall, fishing pressure increases again as the pelagic species return. This is sustained until the water temperature drops low enough to cause the target species to migrate out of the area.

In 1993, the MARMAP program, funded by NOAA's National Marine Fisheries Service (NMFS) and conducted by NMFS and the South Carolina Department of Natural Resources (SCDNR), established sampling stations at the Gray's Reef sanctuary to monitor reef fish populations. During the trapping periods (July 1993-1995; July 1999-2001; October 2002, 2004-2007, 2009-2011), catches were dominated by black sea bass, followed by scup (*Stenotomus chrysops*), tomtate (*Haemulon aurolineatum*) and pinfish (*Lagodon rhomboides*). Other species commonly caught included spottail pinfish (*Diplodus holbrooki*), gray triggerfish (*Balistes capriscus*), leopard toadfish (*Opsanus

Figure 3. Black sea bass catch at Gray's Reef National Marine Sanctuary through the Marine Monitoring, Assessment and Prediction Program – South Carolina Department of Natural Resources.

pardus*), cubbyu (*Pareques umbrosus*), sharksucker (*Echeneis naucrates*), northern puffer (*Sphoeroides maculates*), bank sea bass (*Centropristis ocyurus*) and blue runner (*Caranx crysos*).

In the Gray's Reef sanctuary, the number of black sea bass caught per trap-hour has fluctuated since 1993, with an increasing trend since 2007 (Figure 3). Estimated abundance of black sea bass at the sanctuary showed a generally increasing trend from 1993 to 2006, followed by a decrease in 2007 and subsequent increases through 2011. The 2011 stock assessment has determined that the black sea bass population is rebuilding and is no longer overfished. This suggests that federal region-wide fishery management measures have a greater influence on status of stock than do sanctuary regulations.

Previous tagging studies of black sea bass indicate high rates of tag returns from recreational fishermen, resulting from high fishing effort within the sanctuary. Tagging and catch-curve analysis from trap survey catches indicate that fishing mortality of black sea bass at the Gray's Reef sanctuary has been as high as or higher than that on other reefs throughout the region. Mean length of black sea bass in trap surveys at the sanctuary has increased since 1993, following similar trends throughout the region (MARMAP unpubl.), and is likely influenced by increases in minimum catch size imposed by the South Atlantic Fishery Management Council (Harris et al. 2005)[2]. There is good and consis-

---

South Atlantic Fishery Management Council regulation changes for black sea bass:

1983: 8-inch minimum size for all
1999: 10-inch minimum size for all (has remained the same for commercial; however, they must have 2-inch mesh in traps)
2006: 11-inch minimum size for recreational
2007: 12-inch minimum size for recreational
2011: (proposed) 13-inch minimum size for recreational

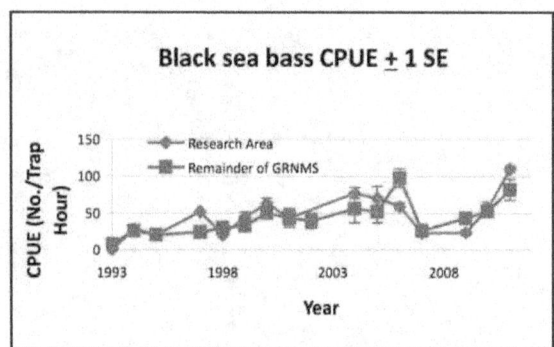

Figure 4. Black sea bass catch per unit effort (CPUE), 1993-2011. Source: Wyanski et al. 2012

Figure 5. One of the two lionfish that were observed for the first time in the sanctuary in fall 2007. Photo: Matt Kendall/NOAA

tent annual recruitment of small black sea bass in trap catches.

Tagging data suggest that most black sea bass tagged within the sanctuary stayed near their release site. Fish that moved out of the sanctuary were significantly larger than those that did not (Sedberry et al. 1998, Barkoukis 2006). Black sea bass distribution in the sanctuary appears to be relatively uniform (Figure 4).

Gag and scamp (*Mycteroperca phenax*) have decreased in abundance in visual census transects, and length-frequency measurements of black sea bass, gag and scamp (from trap and visual census data) indicate that a large portion of the population is removed upon reaching minimum size, either by fishing or by migration out of the sanctuary (Kendall et al. 2008, Wyanski et al. 2012).

There is considerable, but unmeasured, fishing effort on coastal pelagic species (king and Spanish mackerel) during mackerel tournaments and at other times. Federal management of coastal pelagic species has resulted in sustainable fisheries for both mackerel species and the stocks are not currently overfished in the Atlantic. In order to evaluate ecosystem-level impacts on non-targeted species, assessments need to be conducted in the future.

11. What is the status of non-indigenous species and how is it changing?

The status of non-indigenous species in the sanctuary is considered to be "good/fair" — non-indigenous species exist, precluding full community development and function, but are not currently causing substantial or persistent degradation of ecosystem integrity. This trend is declining. Two species of lionfish (*Pterois volitans* and *P. miles*), residents of the western Pacific and eastern Indian oceans only, have become well established in the western Atlantic along the eastern coast of the U.S. (Whitfield et al. 2002, Schofield 2009, http://nas.er.usgs.gov/taxgroup/fish/lionfishdistri-

bution.aspx). In fall 2007, NOAA's National Centers for Coastal Ocean Science reported the first sighting of two red lionfish in the sanctuary (Figure 5) (because very few physical characteristics distinguish the two species of lionfish, it is unknown which species was actually sighted). In December 2011, sanctuary divers sighted another lionfish within the sanctuary, although none were observed during an extensive visual survey in June 2011. So, while lionfish have been regularly observed in close proximity and within the Gray's Reef sanctuary, they have not yet become established in the sanctuary. The range and abundance of these species is considered to be rapidly increasing in the region (Ruiz-Carus et al. 2006, Morris and Whitfield 2009).

In January 2008, three barnacles of the invasive species *Megabalanus coccopoma* (titan acorn barnacle) were found in Gray's Reef attached to the data buoy. Extensive benthic surveys conducted in summer 2011 did not observe *M. coccopoma* on the hard bottom. These barnacles, native to the western Pacific, have been found throughout the western Atlantic along the eastern coast of the U.S. Although not encountered on natural substrates in the sanctuary, monitoring for their presence should be continued.

The benthic surveys conducted in summer 2011 encountered several unrecognized species of tunicates. This group of organisms is known to have high invasion potential (Locke and Carmen 2009), so further investigation, including verification of the species identity of the unrecognized individuals, is warranted. The Asian green mussel (*Perna viridis*) and the orange cup coral (*Tubastraea coccinea*) have both been observed attached to the Gray's Reef data buoy, but have not been observed on live-bottom habitat (McFall, GRNMS, pers. comm.).

Potential impacts of these and other organisms include competition with native species for food and space, predation on native species, and the introduction of diseases or parasites to which native species have no resistance (Ruiz-Carus et al. 2006). Impacts from lionfish could include direct competition with large groupers (*Mycteroperca* and *Epinephelus* spp.) for food, and predation on juvenile stages of fishery species, smaller sea basses (Serranidae spp.) and other benthic fish and crustaceans (Ruiz-Carus et al. 2006, Muñoz et al. 2011). Potential human impacts could result from fishers or divers coming in contact with venomous spines. Impacts from titan barnacles, Asian green mussel and orange cup coral are most likely to involve spatial dominance of available habitat. Titan acorn barnacles could exclude other epifaunal species, including local barnacles, mussels, oysters, corals and sponges. Cold seasonal water temperatures could hinder year-round establishment of lionfish (Kimball et al. 2004).

12. What is the status of key species and how is it changing?

The status of key species in the sanctuary is considered to be "good/fair," based on recent improvements in black sea bass and red snapper populations, as well as king mackerel and grouper. The trend is "improving." The improvement in both ratings since 2008 is based on new data for these species (Question 12 received a status rating of "fair" and a trend rating of "declining" in the 2008 Condition Report). Key species of fishes in the sanctuary include gag, scamp, king mackerel, black sea bass and red snapper, all of which are targeted by fishers and are dominant predators in the ecosystem. Even though populations and average sizes appear to be increasing, they are not found in the numbers that might be anticipated based on the abundance of suitable habitat and available resources (Kendall et al. 2007). Pressure on king mackerel had been steadily increasing at Gray's Reef in the recent past, with the majority of effort coming from fishing tournaments, but this trend appears to have decreased since the last condition report was published.

Direct impacts of fishing within the sanctuary (and the cascading effects on sanctuary resources), in addition to impacts of fishing outside the sanctuary, translate into population responses of fishes within the sanctuary. For example, fishing pressure on species such as greater amberjack (*Seriola dumerili*) throughout the region likely affects the number of this transient species within Gray's Reef and the functional role it plays in mediating indirect interactions between pelagic and demersal piscivores (Auster et al. 2009).

Red snapper (SEDAR 2010a) and red grouper (SEDAR 2010b) are overfished and undergoing overfishing throughout the region. Gag and black sea bass (SEDAR 2011) are undergoing overfishing, but are not overfished throughout the southern Atlantic (NMFS 2012). Previous tagging studies of black sea bass indicated high rates of tag returns from recreational fishermen, reflecting high fishing effort within the sanctuary. The high rate of tag

returns from Gray's Reef also suggests that black sea bass exhibit some degree of site specificity within the sanctuary. Tagging and catch-curve analysis from trap survey catches indicate that fishing mortality for black sea bass at the Gray's Reef sanctuary has been as high as or higher than that on other reefs throughout the region. Mean length of black sea bass in trap surveys at the sanctuary has increased since 1993, following similar trends throughout the region, and is likely influenced by increases in minimum catch size imposed by the South Atlantic Fishery Management Council (Harris et al. 2005, Wyanski et al. 2012). There is good and consistent annual recruitment of small black sea bass in trap catches.

Since August 2008, the overfished/overfishing status of red snapper has not changed. In August 2008, black sea bass and red grouper were listed as experiencing overfishing, the overfished status of red grouper was unknown, and black sea bass was overfished. Since 2008, stock assessments have been conducted on red grouper and black sea bass. A 2009 stock assessment for red grouper determined that the stock is experiencing overfishing and is overfished. However, a four-month spawning season closure for shallow-water groupers implemented in 2009 may be sufficient to end red grouper overfishing and rebuild the stock by 2020. Increasing abundance and size of black sea bass show that increased regulations by the SAFMC and NOAA Fisheries, as mandated by the Magnuson-Stevens Fishery Conservation and Management Act (MSA), are resulting in a positive trend for the species. A stock assessment completed in 2011 indicated black sea bass is undergoing overfishing to a small extent. Furthermore, the 2011 stock assessment has determined that the black sea bass population is rebuilding and is no longer overfished. The black sea bass stock is expected to be rebuilt by 2016.

Benthic cover of invertebrates on live-bottom areas in the sanctuary is dominated by various species of sponges (primarily in the genera *Ircinia* and *Chondrilla*), corals (predominately *Oculina arbuscula* and *Phyllangia americana*), tunicates (including *Styela*, *Aplidium* and *Symplegma*), arborescent bryozoans (primarily *Schizoporella*), bushy hydrozoans (mostly *Eudendrium*), and gorgonians (dominated by *Telesto* and *Leptogorgia*) (Ruzicka 2005, Freeman et al. 2007, Gleason et al. 2007, Ruzicka and Gleason 2009). The abundance of several of these key species — especially *Styela*, *Symplegma* and *Eudendrium* — varies seasonally, with the greatest dominance mid-summer to late-fall. No evidence of disease has been observed in these key benthic species. Long-term monitoring (established 2004) of the benthos has noted some fluctuations in percent cover of these key species, but these changes appear to be due primarily to storm impacts (e.g., movement of sediment) or natural seasonal cycles (Gleason, in prep). Benthic species affected by these impacts often exhibit partial mortality and show high rates of recovery if not dislodged from the substrate. In contrast, reestablishment after complete removal can take several years. If key benthic invertebrates species were rated independently, their rating would be good with a stable trend.

13. What is the condition or health of key species and how is it changing?

The condition of key species at the Gray's Reef sanctuary is only now starting to be systematically assessed, so clear trends, while emerging, are not yet evident. Sponges, recognized as key species at Gray's Reef due to their importance in structuring habitat, have been found to contain organic contaminants (PCBs, PAHs etc.) in their tissues. These filtering organisms appear to be accumulating contaminants from the water column (McFall, GRNMS, pers. comm.). Tissues from arc shells, black sea bass and sediments have been used recently to determine the level of contaminants in the sanctuary (Cooksey et al. 2004, Hyland at al. 2006), but the amounts present in the sponge tissues appear to be higher than levels reported from these other sinks. Coral has also been identified as a key species at Gray's Reef, with the most prominent species being *Oculina arbuscula*. This species shows high recruitment rates, and monitoring at adjacent sites outside the sanctuary suggests that physical factors such as sedimentation exert more influence on population sizes of *O. arbuscula* than biotic factors such as larval supply and competition (Gleason, in prep.). Recent studies confirm a negative correlation between sedimentation rates and both survival and growth of *O. arbuscula* juveniles, but the stochastic nature of sedimentation makes it difficult to identify a population trend for this coral species (Divine 2011). Genetic studies indicating that new individuals of *O. arbuscula* result from "local" recruitment (Wagner 2006), combined with the high recruitment rates observed, reflect a reproductively healthy *O. arbuscula* population in the sanctuary. However, insufficient data still exist to determine a clear trend.

14. What are the levels of human activities that may influence living resource quality and how are they changing?

Certain human activities have resulted in measurable living resource impacts, but evidence suggests effects are localized and not widespread; therefore, this question is rated as "fair."

The activities that are most likely to affect living resources at Gray's Reef are recreational bottom fishing (from boats and perhaps illegal spearfishing), diving (recreational and research), certain research activities (e.g., collecting, coring, data collection), anchoring, disposal of marine debris, and coastal development. Observational data suggest that the activity having the most measurable effect on living resources is recreational bottom fishing. Fishing appears to depress the size-frequency distribution for black sea bass, potentially affecting their abundance, fecundity and availability as food for other species. Additional information shows a regional trend for other species, such as gag and scamp, as well. Existing data suggest that approximately 20 percent of fishers at Gray's Reef participate in bottom fishing (Ehler and Leeworthy 2002), but time-series data that might be used for assessing trends are not currently available.

Preliminary data from one ongoing study suggest that evidence of accumulation of certain organic contaminants in sponges likely results from coastal development, but it is not known whether these are at high enough levels to be of concern. Coastal development is certain to continue to increase, making this an activity that should be monitored closely.

Diver impacts, whether they result from research, recreation or illegal spearfishing, are intermittent and generally limited to specific study locations. Similarly, anchoring and marine debris (Bauer et al. 2008, 2010) are concentrated in locations with high visitation, and most impacts have been observed in areas with the highest relief and cover. Of the marine debris surveyed at Gray's Reef, two-thirds is composed of fishing line (usually entangled), which, like other visitation-related activities, is most heavily concentrated in areas of high relief. Observations of marine debris in the sanctuary have been decreasing since 2007 (McFall, GRNMS, pers. comm.), and anchoring has been prohibited in the sanctuary since 2006. Management approaches that have been employed recently seem to be having an effect, and some data suggest that living resource quality may be improving (e.g., reduced incidence of debris, increasing numbers of black seabass). In addition, the poor economy and increases in fuel costs may have reduced the number of trips made to the sanctuary in recent years, which, combined with new fishing regulations, may be reducing the levels of human activities in the sanctuary. Therefore, the trend for this question is now rated as "improving" (Question 14 received a status rating of "fair" and a trend rating of "undetermined" in the 2008 Condition Report).

Living Resources Status & Trends

#	Issue	Rating	Basis for Judgment	Description of Findings
9	Biodiversity	—	High diversity of sessile invertebrates, benthic infaunal invertebrate density and abundance, and algal abundance and diversity.	Biodiversity appears to reflect pristine or near-pristine conditions and promotes ecosystem integrity (full community development and function).
10	Extracted Species	▲	Recent data showing improvements in black sea bass and red snapper; need more data on non-targeted species to assess ecosystem impacts.	Extraction may inhibit full community development and function, and may cause measurable but not severe degradation of ecosystem integrity.
11	Non-indigenous Species	▼	Occasional lionfish sightings in sanctuary since 2007; titan acom barnacle, Asian green mussel and orange cup coral currently only found on manmade structures.	Non-indigenous species exist, precluding full community development and function, but are unlikely to cause substantial or persistent degradation of ecosystem integrity.
12	Key Species Status	▲	Recent improvements in black sea bass and red snapper populations	Selected key or keystone species are at reduced levels, perhaps precluding full community development and function, but substantial or persistent declines are not expected.
13	Key Species Condition	?	Key species tentatively identified but condition and health undetermined; some contaminants detected in sponges, black seabass and arc shells.	N/A
14	Human Activities	▲	Localized within areas of heavy use, with reduced pressure in certain areas due to management actions and the status of the economy, but trend data limited, suggesting a significant monitoring gap.	Selected activities have resulted in measurable living resource impacts, but evidence suggests effects are localized, not widespread.

Status: Good Good/Fair Fair Fair/Poor Poor Undet.

Trends: Improving (▲), Not Changing (—), Getting Worse (▼), Undetermined Trend (?). Question not applicable (N/A)

Maritime Archaeological Resources

There are currently no known shipwrecks in the sanctuary, but the area does contain considerable paleontological resources of both marine and terrestrial origin. These may have important implications with regard to former human occupation of the area and paleoclimate studies, and they indicate a potential for future archaeological finds.

Scattered macro-paleontological resources have been found in the form of fossil scallop beds in the sanctuary. The fossil scallop beds have given direct evidence for past sea levels and temperatures during the last two glacial periods. These scallops, found at several sites in the sanctuary, have been dated to approximately 42,000 to 44,000 years before present and range in size up to 20 centimeters in diameter. The primary importance of the ancient scallop beds is that they shed some light on past climate conditions at Gray's Reef. The presence of these scallops dictates a much colder environment than what is currently found at Gray's Reef today. More systematic study needs to be done of the diversity and richness of fossil mollusk taxa preserved at the site, which would provide greater confidence in determining past sea level and coastal paleoecology. However, findings from the scallop beds are consistent with the recent documentation of iceberg scours on the seafloor off the coast of South Carolina that indicate very different oceanographic conditions existed as recently as 15,000 years ago (Hill et al. 2009). The death assemblage also indicates a potentially rapid rise in the ocean temperature at Gray's Reef that could make the shells proxies for the timing and rate of climate shifts.

An important element of paleontology, micro-paleontological remains such as palymorphs (e.g., ancient spores and pollen) and foraminifera (a large phylum of amoeboid protists that are among the most common marine plankton species) remain understudied at the sanctuary. Palymorphs have been examined by Russell (2009) and by Garrison et al. (2012). Foraminifera (fossil or modern) have not been systematically evaluated. This is ironic, because the dating of the Gray's Reef substrate to the Pliocene was based on the presence of an extinct foraminiferan taxon (Huddleston 1988).

In the scientific community today, there is great interest in accurate hindcasts for Earth's climate that provide real context by which to measure and assess modern climate change. These fossil resources may provide a significant role in understanding future climate change, which makes it a vital task to preserve and monitor these "maritime archaeological, paleontological and prehistoric resources" in the sanctuary, as set forth in the enabling legislation in the National Marine Sanctuaries Act.

Also occasionally discovered at the sanctuary are fossilized terrestrial and marine mammal bone fragments. These bone fragments help to piece together the changes at Gray's Reef as Georgia's shoreline advanced and retreated over geologic time. It has been documented that Gray's Reef was last exposed approximately 7,000 years ago and prior to that had been submerged and exposed many times, allowing both marine and terrestrial animals to live there.

To date, only a few manmade prehistoric artifacts have been recovered at Gray's Reef. These artifacts have been points of interest and discussion over the years, but no archaeological sites have been discovered in association with these finds. It is possible that humans once lived and hunted in the area before submergence. It thus remains a possibility that important undiscovered archaeological material exists at Gray's Reef. Continued research could provide a larger suite of manmade stone or bone artifacts on a scale similar to the fossil mollusks that have been retrieved and used to decipher the paleontological record for Gray's Reef.

Because Gray's Reef does not contain any known maritime archeological resources, responses to the question (15) "*What is the integrity of known maritime archaeological resources and how is it changing?*" and (16) "*Do known maritime archaeological resources pose an environmental hazard and how is this threat changing?*" are not applicable.

17. What are the levels of human activities that may influence maritime archaeological resource quality and how are they changing?

Some potentially relevant human activities exist in the sanctuary that may influence maritime archaeological resource quality, but they do not appear to have had a negative effect to date. For this reason, this question is rated "good/fair" with a "stable" trend. Natural oceanographic forces pose the main danger to the Gray's Reef sanctuary's prehistoric, archaeological and paleontological resources. Erosion due to storms and natu-

ral currents continuously occurs at the bottom, as moving sand exposes and buries the scallop beds and bone fragments. Little can be done to prevent damage to sanctuary resources from these forces except monitor the sites and recover and document any finds as they become exposed. Recreational diving and anchoring at the sanctuary could potentially impact the resources, but since anchoring has been banned within the sanctuary, it is not expected that this will be a major problem.

Maritime Archaeological Resources Status & Trends

#	Issue	Rating	Basis for Judgment	Description of Findings
15	Integrity	N/A	No archaeological evidence, though former human occupation remains a possibility based on paleontological data.	N/A
16	Threat to Environment	N/A	No archaeological evidence, though former human occupation remains a possibility based on paleontological data.	N/A
17	Human Activities	—	Potential for diving and fishing to damage sites.	Some potentially relevant activities exist, but they do not appear to have had a negative effect on maritime archaeological resource integrity.

Status: Good | Good/Fair | Fair | Fair/Poor | Poor | Undet.

Trends: Improving (▲), Not Changing (—), Getting Worse (▼), Undetermined Trend (?), Question not applicable (N/A)

Cited Resources

Atkinson, L.P., J.O. Blanton, E.B. Haines. 1978. Shelf flushing rates based on the distribution of salinity and freshwater in the Georgia bight. Estuar. Coast. Mar. Sci. 7(5):465-472.

Auster, P.J., J. Godfrey, A. Watson, A. Paquette, G. McFall. 2009. Behavior of prey links midwater and demersal piscivorous reef fishes. Neotropical Ichthyology 7(1)109-112.

Auster, P., D. Grenda, J. Godfrey, E. Heupel, S. Auscavitch, J. Mangiafico. 2011. Behavioral observations of Lilliputian piscivores: young-of-year *Sphyraena barracuda* at offshore sub-tropical reefs (NW Atlantic Ocean). Southeastern Naturalist 10:563-569.

Auster, P.J., L. Kracker, V. Price, E. Heupel, G. McFall, D. Grenda. In review. Behavior webs of piscivores at subtropical live-bottom reefs. Bulletin of Marine Science.

Balthis, W.L., J.L. Hyland, C. Cooksey, M.H. Fulton, G. McFall. 2007. Long-term monitoring of ecological conditions in Gray's Reef National Marine Sanctuary: Comparison of soft-bottom benthic assemblages and contaminant levels in sediments and biota in spring 2000 and 2005. NOAA Technical Memorandum NOS NCCOS 68. 29pp. http://graysreef.noaa.gov/science/publications/pdfs/i-03.pdf

Barkoukis, A.M. 2006. A temporal and spatial analysis of fish trap catches within Gray's Reef National Marine Sanctuary, 1993-2005. A thesis submitted in partial fulfillment of the requirements for the degree master of science in environmental studies at the graduate school of the College of Charleston. 92pp.

Bauer, L.J., M.S. Kendall, C.F.G. Jeffrey. 2008. Incidence of marine debris and its relationships with benthic features in Gray's Reef National Marine Sanctuary, Southeast USA. Marine Pollution Bulletin 56:402-413.

Bauer, L.J., M.S. Kendall, G. McFall. 2010. Assessment and monitoring of marine debris in Gray's Reef National Marine Sanctuary. Prepared by National Centers for Coastal Ocean Science (NCCOS) Biogeography Branch and Gray's Reef National Marine Sanctuary (GRNMS). Silver Spring MD. NOAA Technical Memorandum NOS NCCOS 113. 40pp.

Blanton, J.O. 1981. Ocean currents along a nearshore frontal zone on the continental shelf of the southeastern United States. Journal of Physical Oceanography 11(12):1627-37.

Cohen, R.A. and P. Fong. 2006. Using opportunistic green macroalgae as indicators of nitrogen supply and sources to estuaries. Ecol. App. 16(4):1405-1420.

Cooksey, C.J. Hyland, W.L. Balthis, M. Fulton, G. Scott, D. Bearden. 2004. Soft-bottom benthic assemblages and levels of contaminants in sediments and biota at Gray's Reef National Marine Sanctuary and nearby shelf waters off the coast of Georgia (2000 and 2001). NOAA Tech. Memo. NOS NCCOS 6. NOAA National Ocean Service, National Center for Coastal Environmental Health and Bimolecular Research, Charleston, SC. 55pp.

Cooksey, C., J. Harvey, L. Harwell, J. Hyland, J.K. Summers. 2010. Ecological condition of coastal ocean and estuarine waters of the U.S. South Atlantic Bight: 2000-2004. NOAA Technical Memorandum NOS NCCOS 114, NOAA National Ocean Service, Charleston, SC, 29412-9110; and EPA/600/R-10/046, U.S. EPA, Office of Research and Development, National Health and Environmental Effects Research Laboratory, Gulf Ecology Division, Gulf Breeze, FL, 32561. 88pp.

Diaz, R.J. and R. Rosenberg. 1995. Marine benthic hypoxia: A review of its ecological effects and the behavioural responses of benthic macrofauna. Oceanogr. Mar. Biol. Annu. Rev. 33:245-03.

Divine, L.M. 2011. Effects of sediment on post-settlement growth and survival of the scleractinian coral, *oculina arbuscula* (verrill). M.S. Thesis, Georgia Southern University, Stateboro, GA.

Ehler, R. and V.R. Leeworthy. May 2002. A Socioeconomic Overview of Georgia's Marine Related Industries and Activities; NOAA, U.S. Department of Commerce. http://graysreef.noaa.gov/newdraftplan/socioeconomic.pdf

Freeman, C.J., D.F. Gleason, R. Ruzicka, R.W.M. van Soest, A.W. Harvey, G.B. McFall. 2007. A biogeographic comparison of sponge fauna from Gray's Reef National Marine Sanctuary and other hard-bottom reefs of coastal Georgia, U.S.A. *In*: Porifera Research: Biodiversity, Innovation, and Sustainability, M.R. Custodio, G. Lobo-Hajdu, E. Hajdu, G. Muricy (eds.), Rio de Janeiro, Museu Nacional. pp. 319-325.

Frischer, M.E., J.M. Danforth, T.F. Foy, R. Juraske. 2005. Bioluminescent bacteria as indicators of chemical contamination of coastal waters. Journal of Environmental Quality 34(4):1328-1336.

Fry, B., A. Gace, J.W. McClelland. 2003. Chemical indicators of anthropogenic nitrogen loading in four Pacific estuaries. Pacific Science 57(1):77-101.

Garrison, E.G., W. Weaver, S.L. Littman, J. Cook Hale, P.Srivastava. 2012. Late quaternary paleocology and heinrich events at Gray's Reef national Marine Sanctuary, South Atlantic Bight, USA. Southeastern Geology, 48(4):165-184.

Gleason, D.F., A.W. Harvey, S.P. Vives. 2007. A guide to the benthic invertebrates and cryptic fishes of Gray's Reef. Georgia Southern University. http://www.bio.georgiasouthern.edu/gr-inverts/index.html

Greene, A.K. 2008. Invertebrate endofauna associated with sponge and octocoral epifauna at Gray's Reef National Marine Sanctuary off the coast of Georgia. A thesis Submitted in Partial Fulfillment of the Requirements for the Degree of Master of Science in Marine Biology at the Graduate School of the College of Charleston. 133pp.

Halpern, B.S., K.A. Selkoe, F. Micheli, C.V. Kappel. 2007. Evaluating and ranking the vulnerability of global marine ecosystems to anthropogenic threats. Conservation Biology 21(5):1301-1315.

Hare, J.A., H.J. Walsh, K.E. Marancik, D. Score, G.R. Sedberry, R.O. Parker Jr., R.W. Mays. Unpublished MS. Fish fauna of Gray's Reef National Marine Sanctuary and the implications for place-based management. NOAA Mar. Cons. Ser.

Harris, P.J., G.R. Sedberry, H.S. Meister, D.M. Wyanski. 2005. A summary of monitoring and tagging work by the Marine Resources Monitoring and Assessment Program at Gray's Reef National Marine Sanctuary during 2005. Report submitted to Gray's Reef National Marine Sanctuary by Marine Resources Research Institute, South Carolina Department of Natural Resources, Charleston. 10pp.

Hill, J.C., P.T. Gayes, N.W. Driscoll, E.A. Johnstone, G.R. Sedberry. 2008. Iceberg scours along the southern U.S. Atlantic margin. Geology 36:447-450.

Huddleston, P.F. 1988. A revision of the lithostratigraphic units of the coastal plain of Georgia -Miocene through Holocene. Georgia Geological Survey Bulletin 104pp.

Hunt, J.W., B.S. Anderson, B.M. Phillips, R.S. Tjeerdema, H.M. Puckett, V. deVlaming. 1999. Patterns of aquatic toxicity in an agriculturally dominated coastal watershed. Agriculture Ecosystems and Environment 75(1-2):75-91.

Hyland, J.L., L. Balthis, I. Karakassis, P. Magni, A.N. Petrov, J.P. Shine, O. Vestergaard, R.M. Warwick. 2005. Organic carbon content of sediments as an indicator of stress in the marine benthos. Mar. Ecol. Progr. Ser. 295:91-103.

Hyland, J., C. Cooksey, W.L. Balthis, M. Fulton, D. Bearden, G. McFall, M. Kendall. 2006. The soft-bottom macrobenthos of Gray's Reef National Marine Sanctuary and nearby shelf waters off the coast of Georgia, USA. J. Exper. Mar. Biol. Ecol. 330:307-326.

Kendall, M.S., O.P. Jensen, C. Alexander, D. Field, G. McFall, R. Bohne, M.E. Monaco. 2005. Benthic mapping using sonar video transects, and an innovative approach to accurate assessment: A characterization of bottom features in the Georgia Bight. J. Coastal Res. 21:1154-1165.

Kendall, M.S., L.J. Bauer, C.F.G. Jeffrey. 2007. Characterization of the benthos, marine debris and bottom fish at Gray's Reef National Marine Sanctuary. Prepared by National Centers for Coastal Ocean Science (NCCOS) Biogeography Team in cooperation with the National Marine Sanctuary Program. Silver Spring, MD. NOAA Technical Memorandum NOS NCCOS 50. 82 pp. +Appendices.

Kendall, M.S., L.J. Bauer, C.F.G. Jeffrey. 2008. Influence of benthic features and fishing pressures on size and size and distribution of three exploited reef fishes from the southeastern United States. Transactions of the American Fisheries Society 137:1134–1146.

Kendall M.S., L.J. Bauer, C.F.G. Jeffrey. 2009. Influence of hardbottom morphology on fish assemblages of the continental shelf off Georgia, Southeastern USA. Bulletin of Marine Science 84:265-286

Kimball, M.E., J.M. Miller, P.E. Whitfield, J.A. Hare. 2004. Thermal tolerance and potential distribution of invasive lionfish (*Pterois volitans/miles* complex) on the east coast of the United States. Mar. Ecol. Progr. Ser. 283: 269-278.

Li, C. 2001. Penetrating shelf front in the south Atlantic bight. American Geophysical Union Ocean Sciences Meeting, Honolulu, Hawaii (USA), 11-15 Feb 2002. Vol. 82, suppl.

Locke, A. and M. Carman. 2009. An overview of the 2nd international invasive sea squirt conference: what we learned. Aquatic Invasions 4:1-4.

Long, J.D., M.E. Frischer, C.Y. Robertson. 2007. A Phaeocystis globosa bloom associated with upwelling in the subtropical South Atlantic Bight Journal of Plankton Research 2007 29(9):769-774.

McClelland, J.W., I. Valiela, R.H. Michener. 1997. Nitrogen-stable isotope signatures in estuarine food webs: a record of increasing urbanization in coastal watersheds. Limnology and Oceanography 42:930-937.

Morris, J.A., Jr., and P.E. Whitfield. 2009. Biology, ecology, control and management of the invasive Indo-Pacific lionfish: an updated integrated assessment. NOAA Technical Memorandum NOS NCCOS 99. 57pp.

Muñoz, R.C., Currin, C.A., P.E. Whitfield. 2011. Diet of invasive lionfish on hard bottom reefs of the Southeast USA: insights from stomach contents and stable isotopes. Marine Ecology Progress Series 432:181-193.

NMSP (National Marine Sanctuary Program). 2004. A monitoring framework for the National Marine Sanctuary System. U.S. Dept. of Commerce, National Oceanic and Atmospheric Administration, National Ocean Service. Silver Spring, MD. 22pp.

NMSP (National Marine Sanctuary Program). 2006. Gray's Reef National Marine Sanctuary final management plan/final environmental impact statement. U.S. Department of Commerce, National Oceanic and Atmospheric Administration, National Marine Sanctuary Program, Silver Spring, MD. 260pp.

NMFS (National Marine Fisheries Service). 2012. Annual report to congress on the status of U.S. fisheries-2011, U.S. Department of Commerce, NOAA, National Marine Fisheries Service, Silver Spring, MD, 20pp.

ONMS (Office of National Marine Sanctuaries). 2008. Gray's Reef national marine sanctuary condition report 2008. U.S. Department of Commerce, National Oceanic and Atmospheric Administration, Office of National Marine Sanctuaries, Silver Spring, MD. 42pp. http://sanctuaries.noaa.gov/science/condition/grnms

Posey, M.H.,T.D. Alphin, L.B. Cahoon, D.G. Lindquist, M.A. Mallin, M.B. Nevers. 2002. Top-down Versus Bottom-up Limitation in Benthic Infaunal Communities: Direct and Indirect Effects. Estuaries (25)5:999–1014.

Ruiz-Carus, R., R.E. Matheson, D.E. Roberts, P.E. Whitfield. 2006. The western Pacific red lionfish, *Pterois volitans* (Scorpaenidae). *In:* Florida: Evidence for reproduction and parasitism in the first exotic marine fish established in state waters. Biol. Conserv. 128(March):384-390.

Russell, D.A., F.J. Rich, V. Schneider, J. Lynch-Stiegliz. 2009. A warm thermal enclave in the late Pleistocene of the south-eastern United States. Biological Reviews 84:173-202.

Ruzicka, R. 2005. Sponge community structure and anti-predator defenses on temperate reefs of the South Atlantic Bight. M.S. Thesis, Georgia Southern University, Statesboro, GA. 84pp.

Ruzicka, R. and D.F. Gleason. 2008. Latitudinal variation in spongivorous fishes and the effectiveness of sponge chemical defenses. Oecologia 154:785-794.

Ruzicka, R. and D.F. Gleason. 2009. Sponge community structure and anti-predator defenses on temperate reefs of the South Atlantic Bight. Journal of Experimental Marine Biology and Ecology 380:36-46.

Sanamyan, K., D.F. Gleason, N. Sanamyan. 2009. A new species of *Polyzoa* (Ascidiacea: Styelidae) from the Atlantic coast of N. America, U.S.A. Zootaxa 2088:65-68.

Schofield, P. 2009. Geographic extent and chronology of the invasion of non-native lionfish (*Pterois volitans* [Linnaeus 1758] and *P. miles* [Bennett 1828]) in the Western North Atlantic and Caribbean Sea. Aquatic Invasions 4(3)473-479.

Sedberry, G.R., O. Pashuk, D.M. Wyanski, J.A. Stephen, P. Weinbach. 2006. Spawning locations for Atlantic reef fishes off the southeastern U.S. Proc. Gulf Carib. Fish. Inst. 57:463-514.

SEDAR. 2010a. SouthEast Data, Assessment, and Review. SEDAR 24, Stock assessment report, south Atlantic red snapper. October 2010. SEDAR, South Atlantic Fishery Management Council, North Charleston SC. 524pp.

SEDAR. 2010b. Southeast Data, Assessment, and Review. SEDAR 19, Stock assessment report, south Atlantic red grouper. April 2010. SEDAR, South Atlantic Fishery Management Council, North Charleston SC. 612pp.

SEDAR. 2011. Southeast Data, Assessment, and Review. SEDAR 25, stock assessment report, south Atlantic black sea bass. October 2011. SEDAR, South Atlantic Fishery Management Council, North Charleston SC. 480pp.

Tenore, K.R., C.F. Chamberlain, W.M. Dunstan, R.B. Hanson, B. Sherr, J.H. Tietjen. 1978. Possible effects of Gulf Stream intrusions and coastal runoff on the benthos of the continental shelf of the Georgia Bight. *In:* M.L. Wiley (ed.) Estuarine interactions. Academic Press, New York, pp. 577-598.

Thompson, B., R. Hoenicke, J. Davis, A. Gunther. 2000. An overview of contaminant-related issues identified by monitoring in San Francisco Bay. Environmental Monitoring and Assessment 64(1):409-419.

Verity, P.G., M. Alber, S.B. Bricker. 2006. Development of hypoxia in well-mixed subtropical estuaries in the southeastern USA. Estuaries and Coasts 29(4):665-673.

Visser, J.M., C.E. Sasser, R.H. Chabreck, R.G. Linscombe. 2002. The impact of a severe drought on the vegetation of a subtropical estuary. Estuaries 25(6A):1184-95.

Wagner, L.M. 2006. Population genetic structure of the temperate scleractinian coral, *Oculina arbuscula*, in coastal Georgia. M.S. Thesis, Georgia Southern University, 59pp.

Walker S.E., R.M. Dickhut, C. Chisholm-Brause. 2004. Polycyclic aromatic hydrocarbons in a highly industrialized urban estuary. Environmental Toxicology and Chemistry 23(11):2655-2664.

Whitfield, P.E., T. Gardner, S.P. Vives, M.R. Gilligan, W.R. Coutenay Jr., G.C. Ray, J.A. Hare. 2002. Biological invasion of the Indo-Pacific lionfish *Pterois volitans* along the Atlantic coast of North America. Mar. Ecol. Prog. Ser. 235:289-297.

Wyanski, D.M., M.J.M. Reichert, S.M. Pate. 2012. A summary of reef fish monitoring by the Marine Resources Monitoring and Assessment Program at Gray's Reef National Marine Sanctuary during 2011. MARMAP Technical Report #2012-019.

Additional Resources

Georgia Department of Natural Resources: http://www.gadnr.org

Gray's Reef National Marine Sanctuary: http://graysreef.noaa.gov

National Oceanic and Atmospheric Administration (NOAA): http://www.noaa.gov

NOAA Marine Debris Program: http://marinedebris.noaa.gov

NOAA National Marine Fisheries Service: http://www.nmfs.noaa.gov

NOAA National Marine Protected Areas Center: http://www.mpa.gov

NOAA Ocean Explorer, South Atlantic Bight: http://oceanexplorer.noaa.gov/explorations/islands01/background/bight/bight.html

NOAA Ocean Explorer: http://www.oceanexplorer.noaa.gov

NOAA Office of National Marine Sanctuaries: http://sanctuaries.noaa.gov

NOAA Southeast Fisheries Science Center: http://www.sefsc.noaa.gov

Reef Environmental Education Foundation: http://www.reef.org

Sherpa Guides, The Natural History of Georgia's Barrier Islands: http://sherpaguides.com/georgia/barrier_islands/natural_history

Skidaway Institute of Oceanography: http://www.skio.usg.edu

South Atlantic Bight Synoptic Offshore Observational Network: http://www.skio.peachnet.edu/research/sabsoon

South Atlantic Fishery Management Council: http://www.safmc.net

USGS Nonindigenous Aquatic Species: http://nas.er.usgs.gov

Woods Hole Oceanographic Institution: http://www.whoi.edu

Appendix: Rating Scheme for System-Wide Monitoring Questions

The purpose of this appendix is to clarify the 17 questions and possible responses used to report the condition of sanctuary resources in "Condition Reports" for all national marine sanctuaries. Individual staff and partners utilized this guidance, as well as their own informed and detailed understanding of the site to make judgments about the status and trends of sanctuary resources.

The questions derive from the National Marine Sanctuary System's mission, and a system-wide monitoring framework (NMSP 2004) developed to ensure the timely flow of data and information to those responsible for managing and protecting resources in the ocean and coastal zone, and to those that use, depend on and study the ecosystems encompassed by the sanctuaries[3]. They are being used to guide staff and partners at each of the 14 sites in the sanctuary system in the development of this first periodic sanctuary condition report. Evaluations of status and trends may be based on interpretation of quantitative and, when necessary, non-quantitative assessments and observations of scientists, managers and users.

Ratings for a number of questions depend on judgments involving "ecological integrity," and an ecosystem's status with regard to it. This is because one of the foundational principles behind the establishment of marine sanctuaries is to protect ocean ecosystems. But this concept can be confusing, and is interpreted in different ways, so it is important to provide clarification of its application within this report. Ecological integrity implies the presence of naturally occurring species, populations and communities, and ecological processes functioning at appropriate rates, scales, and levels of natural variation, as well as the environmental conditions that support these attributes (modified from National Park Service Vital Signs monitoring program: http://science.nature.nps.gov/im/monitor/Glossary.cfm). Ecosystems have integrity when they have their native components intact, including abiotic components (the physical elements, such as water and habitats), biodiversity (the composition and abundance of species and communities in an ecosystem), and ecosystem processes (the engines that makes ecosystem work (e.g., space competition, predation, symbioses) (from Parks Canada at http://www.pc.gc.ca/progs/np-pn/ie-ei.aspx). For purposes of this report, the level of integrity that is judged to exist is based on the extent to which humans have altered key attributes, and the effect of that change on the ability of an ecosystem to resist continued change and recover from it. The statements for many questions are intended to reflect this judgment. Reference is made in the rating system to "near-pristine" conditions, which for this report would imply a status as near to an unaltered ecosystem as we can reasonably presume to exist, recognizing that there are virtually no ecosystems on Earth completely free from human influence.

Not all questions, however, use ecological integrity as a basis for judgment. One focuses on the impacts of water quality factors on human health. Another rates the status of key species compared with that expected in an unaltered ecosystem. One rates maritime archaeological resources based on their historical, archaeological, scientific, and educational value. Another considers the level and persistence of localized threats posed by degrading archaeological resources. Finally, four ask specifically about the levels of on-going human activity that could affect resource condition.

During workshops in which status and trends are rated, experts discuss each question, and relevant data, literature, and experience associated with the topic. They then discuss statements that are presented as options for judgments about the status. These statements have been customized for each question. Once a particular statement is agreed upon, a color code and status rating (e.g., good, fair, poor) is assigned. Experts can also decide that the most appropriate rating " N/A" (the question does not apply) or "Undet." (resource status is undetermined).

A subsequent discussion is then held about the trend and whether conditions are improving, remaining the same, or declining. Symbols used to indicate trends are the same for all questions: "▲ " – conditions appear to be improving; "—" – conditions do not appear to be changing; "▼ " – conditions appear to be declining; and "?" – trend is undetermined.

---

[3]In 2012 the Office of National Marine Sanctuaries led an effort to review and revise the set of questions and their possible responses posed in the Condition Reports. The revised questions are not reflected in the 2012 Gray's Reef National Marine Sanctuary Condition Report Addendum. The revised questions will be addressed when the Condition Report in its entirety is revised in the future.

Water Stressors

1. Are specific or multiple stressors, including changing oceanographic and atmospheric conditions, affecting water quality and how are they changing?

This is meant to capture shifts in condition arising from certain changing physical processes and anthropogenic inputs. Factors resulting in regionally accelerated rates of change in water temperature, salinity, dissolved oxygen, or water clarity, could all be judged to reduce water quality. Localized changes in circulation or sedimentation resulting, for example, from coastal construction or dredge spoil disposal, can affect light penetration, salinity regimes, oxygen levels, productivity, waste transport, and other factors that influence habitat and living resource quality. Human inputs, generally in the form of contaminants from point or non-point sources, including fertilizers, pesticides, hydrocarbons, heavy metals, and sewage, are common causes of environmental degradation, often in combination rather than alone. Certain biotoxins, such as domoic acid, may be of particular interest to specific sanctuaries. When present in the water column, any of these contaminants can affect marine life by direct contact or ingestion, or through bioaccumulation via the food chain.

[Note: Over time, accumulation in sediments can sequester and concentrate contaminants. Their effects may manifest only when the sediments are resuspended during storm or other energetic events. In such cases, reports of status should be made under Question 7 – Habitat contaminants.]

Good	Conditions do not appear to have the potential to negatively affect living resources or habitat quality.
Good/Fair	Selected conditions may preclude full development of living resource assemblages and habitats, but are not likely to cause substantial or persistent declines.
Fair	Selected conditions may inhibit the development of assemblages, and may cause measurable but not severe declines in living resources and habitats.
Fair/Poor	Selected conditions have caused or are likely to cause severe declines in some but not all living resources and habitats.
Poor	Selected conditions have caused or are likely to cause severe declines in most if not al, living resources and habitats.

Water Eutrophic Condition

2. What is the eutrophic condition of sanctuary waters and how is it changing?

Nutrient enrichment often leads to planktonic and/or benthic algae blooms. Some affect benthic communities directly through space competition. Overgrowth and other competitive interactions (e.g., accumulation of algal-sediment mats) often lead to shifts in dominance in the benthic assemblage. Disease incidence and frequency can also be affected by algae competition and the resulting chemistry along competitive boundaries. Blooms can also affect water column conditions, including light penetration and plankton availability, which can alter pelagic food webs. Harmful algal blooms often affect resources, as biotoxins are released into the water and air, and oxygen can be depleted.

Good	Conditions do not appear to have the potential to negatively affect living resources or habitat quality.
Good/Fair	Selected conditions may preclude full development of living resource assemblages and habitats, but are not likely to cause substantial or persistent declines.
Fair	Selected conditions may inhibit the development of assemblages, and may cause measurable but not severe declines in living resources and habitats.
Fair/Poor	Selected conditions have caused or are likely to cause severe declines in some but not all living resources and habitats.
Poor	Selected conditions have caused or are likely to cause severe declines in most if not all living resources and habitats.

Water
Human Health

3. | **Do sanctuary waters pose risks to human health and how are they changing?**

Human health concerns are generally aroused by evidence of contamination (usually bacterial or chemical) in bathing waters or fish intended for consumption. They also emerge when harmful algal blooms are reported or when cases of respiratory distress or other disorders attributable to harmful algal blooms increase dramatically. Any of these conditions should be considered in the course of judging the risk to humans posed by waters in a marine sanctuary.

Some sites may have access to specific information on beach and shellfish conditions. In particular, beaches may be closed when criteria for safe water body contact are exceeded, or shellfish harvesting may be prohibited when contaminant loads or infection rates exceed certain levels. These conditions can be evaluated in the context of the descriptions below.

	Good	Conditions do not appear to have the potential to negatively affect human health.
	Good/Fair	Selected conditions that have the potential to affect human health may exist but human impacts have not been reported.
	Fair	Selected conditions have resulted in isolated human impacts, but evidence does not justify widespread or persistent concern.
	Fair/Poor	Selected conditions have caused or are likely to cause severe impacts, but cases to date have not suggested a pervasive problem.
	Poor	Selected conditions warrant widespread concern and action, as large-scale, persistent, and/or repeated severe impacts are likely or have occurred.

Water
Human Activities

4. | **What are the levels of human activities that may influence water quality and how are they changing?**

Among the human activities in or near sanctuaries that affect water quality are those involving direct discharges (transiting vessels, visiting vessels, onshore and offshore industrial facilities, public wastewater facilities), those that contribute contaminants to stream, river, and water control discharges (agriculture, runoff from impermeable surfaces through storm drains, conversion of land use), and those releasing airborne chemicals that subsequently deposit via particulates at sea (vessels, land-based traffic, power plants, manufacturing facilities, refineries). In addition, dredging and trawling can cause resuspension of contaminants in sediments.

	Good	Few or no activities occur that are likely to negatively affect water quality.
	Good/Fair	Some potentially harmful activities exist, but they do not appear to have had a negative effect on water quality.
	Fair	Selected activities have resulted in measurable resource impacts, but evidence suggests effects are localized, not widespread.
	Fair/Poor	Selected activities have caused or are likely to cause severe impacts, and cases to date suggest a pervasive problem.
	Poor	Selected activities warrant widespread concern and action, as large-scale, persistent, and/or repeated severe impacts have occurred or are likely to occur.

Habitat
Abundance &
Distribution

5. | **What are the abundance and distribution of major habitat types and how are they changing?**

Habitat loss is of paramount concern when it comes to protecting marine and terrestrial ecosystems. Of greatest concern to sanctuaries are changes caused, either directly or indirectly, by human activities. The loss of shoreline is recognized as a problem indirectly caused by human activities. Habitats with submerged aquatic vegetation are often altered by changes in water conditions in estuaries, bays, and nearshore waters. Intertidal zones can be affected for long periods by spills or by chronic pollutant exposure. Beaches and haul-out areas can be littered with dangerous marine debris, as can the water column or benthic habitats. Sandy subtidal areas and hardbottoms are frequently disturbed or destroyed by trawling. Even rocky areas several hundred meters deep are increasingly affected by certain types of trawls, bottom longlines and fish traps. Groundings, anchors and divers damage submerged reefs. Cables and pipelines disturb corridors across numerous habitat types and can be destructive if they become mobile. Shellfish dredging removes, alters and fragments habitats.

The result of these activities is the gradual reduction of the extent and quality of marine habitats. Losses can often be quantified through visual surveys and to some extent using high-resolution mapping. This question asks about the quality of habitats compared to those that would be expected without human impacts. The status depends on comparison to a baseline that existed in the past - one toward which restoration efforts might aim.

Good	Habitats are in pristine or near-pristine condition and are unlikely to preclude full community development.
Good/Fair	Selected habitat loss or alteration has taken place, precluding full development of living resource assemblages, but it is unlikely to cause substantial or persistent degradation in living resources or water quality.
Fair	Selected habitat loss or alteration may inhibit the development of assemblages, and may cause measurable but not severe declines in living resources or water quality.
Fair/Poor	Selected habitat loss or alteration has caused or is likely to cause severe declines in some but not all living resources or water quality.
Poor	Selected habitat loss or alteration has caused or is likely to cause severe declines in most if not all living resources or water quality.

Habitat
Structure

6. | **What is the condition of biologically structured habitats and how is it changing?**

Many organisms depend on the integrity of their habitats and that integrity is largely determined by the condition of particular living organisms. Coral reefs may be the best known examples of such biologically-structured habitats. Not only is the substrate itself biogenic, but the diverse assemblages residing within and on the reefs depend on and interact with each other in tightly linked food webs. They also depend on each other for the recycling of wastes, hygiene, and the maintenance of water quality, among other requirements.

Kelp beds may not be biogenic habitats to the extent of coral reefs, but kelp provides essential habitat for assemblages that would not reside or function together without it. There are other communities of organisms that are also similarly co-dependent, such as hard-bottom communities, which may be structured by bivalves, octocorals, coralline algae, or other groups that generate essential habitat for other species. Intertidal assemblages structured by mussels, barnacles, and algae are another example, seagrass beds another. This question is intended to address these types of places, where organisms form structures (habitats) on which other organisms depend.

Good	Habitats are in pristine or near-pristine condition and are unlikely to preclude full community development.
Good/Fair	Selected habitat loss or alteration has taken place, precluding full development of living resources, but it is unlikely to cause substantial or persistent degradation in living resources or water quality.
Fair	Selected habitat loss or alteration may inhibit the development of living resources, and may cause measurable but not severe declines in living resources or water quality.
Fair/Poor	Selected habitat loss or alteration has caused or is likely to cause severe declines in some but not all living resources or water quality.
Poor	Selected habitat loss or alteration has caused or is likely to cause severe declines in most if not all living resources or water quality.

Habitat
Contaminants

7. | **What are the contaminant concentrations in sanctuary habitats and how are they changing?**

This question addresses the need to understand the risk posed by contaminants within benthic formations, such as soft sediments, hard bottoms, or biogenic organisms. In the first two cases, the contaminants can become available when released via disturbance. They can also pass upwards through the food chain after being ingested by bottom dwelling prey species. The contaminants of concern generally include pesticides, hydrocarbons, and heavy metals, but the specific concerns of individual sanctuaries may differ substantially.

■	Good	Contaminants do not appear to have the potential to negatively affect living resources or water quality.
▨	Good/Fair	Selected contaminants may preclude full development of living resource assemblages, but are not likely to cause substantial or persistent degradation.
	Fair	Selected contaminants may inhibit the development of assemblages, and may cause measurable but not severe declines in living resources or water quality.
▨	Fair/Poor	Selected contaminants have caused or are likely to cause severe declines in some but not all living resources or water quality.
■	Poor	Selected contaminants have caused or are likely to cause severe declines in most if not all living resources or water quality.

Habitat
Human Activities

8. | **What are the levels of human activities that may influence habitat quality and how are they changing?**

Human activities that degrade habitat quality do so by affecting structural (geological), biological, oceanographic, acoustic, or chemical characteristics. Structural impacts include removal or mechanical alteration, including various fishing techniques (trawls, traps, dredges, longlines, and even hook-and-line in some habitats), dredging channels and harbors and dumping spoil, vessel groundings, anchoring, laying pipelines and cables, installing offshore structures, discharging drill cuttings, dragging tow cables, and placing artificial reefs. Removal or alteration of critical biological components of habitats can occur along with several of the above activities, most notably trawling, groundings, and cable drags. Marine debris, particularly in large quantities (e.g., lost gillnets and other types of fishing gear), can affect both biological and structural habitat components. Changes in water circulation often occur when channels are dredged, fill is added, coastal areas are reinforced, or other construction takes place. These activities affect habitat by changing food delivery, waste removal, water quality (e.g., salinity, clarity and sedimentation), recruitment patterns, and a host of other factors. Acoustic impacts can occur to water column habitats and organisms from acute and chronic sources of anthropogenic noise (e.g., shipping, boating, construction). Chemical alterations most commonly occur following spills and can have both acute and chronic impacts.

■	Good	Few or no activities occur that are likely to negatively affect habitat quality.
▨	Good/Fair	Some potentially harmful activities exist, but they do not appear to have had a negative effect on habitat quality.
	Fair	Selected activities have resulted in measurable habitat impacts, but evidence suggests effects are localized, not widespread.
▨	Fair/Poor	Selected activities have caused or are likely to cause severe impacts, and cases to date suggest a pervasive problem.
■	Poor	Selected activities warrant widespread concern and action, as large-scale, persistent, and/or repeated severe impacts have occurred or are likely to occur.

Living Resources
Biodiversity

9. | **What is the status of biodiversity and how is it changing?**

This is intended to elicit thought and assessment of the condition of living resources based on expected biodiversity levels and the interactions between species. Intact ecosystems require that all parts not only exist, but that they function together, resulting in natural symbioses, competition, and predator-prey relationships. Community integrity, resistance and resilience all depend on these relationships. Abundance, relative abundance, trophic structure, richness, H' diversity, evenness, and other measures are often used to assess these attributes.

Good Biodiversity appears to reflect pristine or near-pristine conditions and promotes ecosystem integrity (full community development and function).

Good/Fair Selected biodiversity loss has taken place, precluding full community development and function, but it is unlikely to cause substantial or persistent degradation of ecosystem integrity.

Fair Selected biodiversity loss may inhibit full community development and function, and may cause measurable but not severe degradation of ecosystem integrity.

Fair/Poor Selected biodiversity loss has caused or is likely to cause severe declines in some but not all ecosystem components and reduce ecosystem integrity.

Poor Selected biodiversity loss has caused or is likely to cause severe declines in ecosystem integrity.

Living Resources
Extracted Species

10. | **What is the status of environmentally sustainable fishing and how is it changing?**

Commercial and recreational harvesting are highly selective activities, for which fishers and collectors target a limited number of species, and often remove high proportions of populations. In addition to removing significant amounts of biomass from the ecosystem, reducing its availability to other consumers, these activities tend to disrupt specific and often critical food web links. When too much extraction occurs (i.e. ecologically unsustainable harvesting), trophic cascades ensue, resulting in changes in the abundance of non-targeted species as well. It also reduces the ability of the targeted species to replenish populations at a rate that supports continued ecosystem integrity.

It is essential to understand whether removals are occurring at ecologically sustainable levels. Knowing extraction levels and determining the impacts of removal are both ways that help gain this understanding. Measures for target species of abundance, catch amounts or rates (e.g., catch per unit effort), trophic structure, and changes in non-target species abundance are all generally used to assess these conditions.

Other issues related to this question include whether fishers are using gear that is compatible with the habitats being fished and whether that gear minimizes by-catch and incidental take of marine mammals. For example, bottom-tending gear often destroys or alters both benthic structure and non-targeted animal and plant communities. "Ghost fishing" occurs when lost traps continue to capture organisms. Lost or active nets, as well as lines used to mark and tend traps and other fishing gear, can entangle marine mammals. Any of these could be considered indications of environmentally unsustainable fishing techniques.

Good Extraction does not appear to affect ecosystem integrity (full community development and function).

Good/Fair Extraction takes place, precluding full community development and function, but it is unlikely to cause substantial or persistent degradation of ecosystem integrity.

Fair Extraction may inhibit full community development and function, and may cause measurable but not severe degradation of ecosystem integrity.

Fair/Poor Extraction has caused or is likely to cause severe declines in some but not all ecosystem components and reduce ecosystem integrity.

Poor Extraction has caused or is likely to cause severe declines in ecosystem integrity.

Living Resources
Non-Indigenous Species

11. | What is the status of non-indigenous species and how is it changing?

Non-indigenous species are generally considered problematic, and candidates for rapid response, if found, soon after invasion. For those that become established, their impacts can sometimes be assessed by quantifying changes in the affected native species. This question allows sanctuaries to report on the threat posed by non-indigenous species. In some cases, the presence of a species alone constitutes a significant threat (certain invasive algae). In other cases, impacts have been measured, and may or may not significantly affect ecosystem integrity.

Good — Non-indigenous species are not suspected or do not appear to affect ecosystem integrity (full community development and function).

Good/Fair — Non-indigenous species exist, precluding full community development and function, but are unlikely to cause substantial or persistent degradation of ecosystem integrity.

Fair — Non-indigenous species may inhibit full community development and function, and may cause measurable but not severe degradation of ecosystem integrity.

Fair/Poor — Non-indigenous species have caused or are likely to cause severe declines in some but not all ecosystem components and reduce ecosystem integrity.

Poor — Non-indigenous species have caused or are likely to cause severe declines in ecosystem integrity.

Living Resources
Key Species

12. | What is the status of key species and how is it changing?

Certain species can be defined as "key" within a marine sanctuary. Some might be keystone species, that is, species on which the persistence of a large number of other species in the ecosystem depends - the pillar of community stability. Their functional contribution to ecosystem function is disproportionate to their numerical abundance or biomass and their impact is therefore important at the community or ecosystem level. Their removal initiates changes in ecosystem structure and sometimes the disappearance of or dramatic increase in the abundance of dependent species. Keystone species may include certain habitat modifiers, predators, herbivores, and those involved in critical symbiotic relationships (e.g. cleaning or co-habitating species).

Other key species may include those that are indicators of ecosystem condition or change (e.g., particularly sensitive species), those targeted for special protection efforts, or charismatic species that are identified with certain areas or ecosystems. These may or may not meet the definition of keystone, but do require assessments of status and trends.

Good — Key and keystone species appear to reflect pristine or near-pristine conditions and may promote ecosystem integrity (full community development and function).

Good/Fair — Selected key or keystone species are at reduced levels, perhaps precluding full community development and function, but substantial or persistent declines are not expected.

Fair — The reduced abundance of selected keystone species may inhibit full community development and function, and may cause measurable but not severe degradation of ecosystem integrity; or selected key species are at reduced levels, but recovery is possible.

Fair/Poor — The reduced abundance of selected keystone species has caused or is likely to cause severe declines in some but not all ecosystem components, and reduce ecosystem integrity; or selected key species are at substantially reduced levels, and prospects for recovery are uncertain.

Poor — The reduced abundance of selected keystone species has caused or is likely to cause severe declines in ecosystem integrity; or selected key species are a severely reduced levels, and recovery is unlikely.

Living Resources
Health of Key
Species

13. | What is the condition or health of key species and how is it changing?

For those species considered essential to ecosystem integrity, measures of their condition can be important to determining the likelihood that they will persist and continue to provide vital ecosystem functions. Measures of condition may include growth rates, fecundity, recruitment, age-specific survival, tissue contaminant levels, pathologies (disease incidence tumors, deformities), the presence and abundance of critical symbionts, or parasite loads. Similar measures of condition may also be appropriate for other key species (indicator, protected, or charismatic species). In contrast to the question about keystone species (#12 above), the impact of changes in the abundance or condition of key species is more likely to be observed at the population or individual level, and less likely to result in ecosystem or community effects.

Good	The condition of key resources appears to reflect pristine or near-pristine conditions.
Good/Fair	The condition of selected key resources is not optimal, perhaps precluding full ecological function, but substantial or persistent declines are not expected.
Fair	The diminished condition of selected key resources may cause a measurable but not severe reduction in ecological function, but recovery is possible.
Fair/Poor	The comparatively poor condition of selected key resources makes prospects for recovery uncertain.
Poor	The poor condition of selected key resources makes recovery unlikely.

Living Resources
Human Activities

14. | What are the levels of human activities that may influence living resource quality and how are they changing?

Human activities that degrade living resource quality do so by causing a loss or reduction of one or more species, by disrupting critical life stages, by impairing various physiological processes, or by promoting the introduction of non-indigenous species or pathogens. (Note: Activities that impact habitat and water quality may also affect living resources. These activities are dealt with in Questions 4 and 8, and many are repeated here as they also have direct effect on living resources).

Fishing and collecting are the primary means of removing resources. Bottom trawling, seine-fishing, and the collection of ornamental species for the aquarium trade are all common examples, some being more selective than others. Chronic mortality can be caused by marine debris derived from commercial or recreational vessel traffic, lost fishing gear, and excess visitation, resulting in the gradual loss of some species.

Critical life stages can be affected in various ways. Mortality to adult stages is often caused by trawling and other fishing techniques, cable drags, dumping spoil or drill cuttings, vessel groundings, or persistent anchoring. Contamination of areas by acute or chronic spills, discharges by vessels, or municipal and industrial facilities can make them unsuitable for recruitment; the same activities can make nursery habitats unsuitable. Although coastal armoring and construction can increase the availability of surfaces suitable for the recruitment and growth of hard bottom species, the activity may disrupt recruitment patterns for other species (e.g., intertidal soft bottom animals) and habitat may be lost.

Spills, discharges, and contaminants released from sediments (e.g., by dredging and dumping) can all cause physiological impairment and tissue contamination. Such activities can affect all life stages by reducing fecundity, increasing larval, juvenile, and adult mortality, reducing disease resistance, and increasing susceptibility to predation. Bioaccumulation allows some contaminants to move upward through the food chain, disproportionately affecting certain species.

Activities that promote introductions include bilge discharges and ballast water exchange, commercial shipping and vessel transportation. Releases of aquarium fish can also lead to species introductions.

Good	Few or no activities occur that are likely to negatively affect living resource quality.
Good/Fair	Some potentially harmful activities exist, but they do not appear to have had a negative effect on living resource quality.
Fair	Selected activities have resulted in measurable living resource impacts, but evidence suggests effects are localized, not widespread.
Fair/Poor	Selected activities have caused or are likely to cause severe impacts, and cases to date suggest a pervasive problem.
Poor	Selected activities warrant widespread concern and action, as large-scale, persistent, and/or repeated severe impacts have occurred or are likely to occur.

Maritime Archaeological Resources Integrity

15. **What is the integrity of known maritime archaeological resources and how is it changing?**

The condition of archaeological resources in a marine sanctuary significantly affects their value for science and education, as well as the resource's eligibility for listing in the National Register of Historic Places. Assessments of archaeological sites include evaluation of the apparent levels of site integrity, which are based on levels of previous human disturbance and the level of natural deterioration. The historical, scientific and educational values of sites are also evaluated, and are substantially determined and affected by site condition.

Good
: Known archaeological resources appear to reflect little or no unexpected disturbance.

Good/Fair
: Selected archaeological resources exhibit indications of disturbance, but there appears to have been little or no reduction in historical, scientific, or educational value.

Fair
: The diminished condition of selected archaeological resources has reduced, to some extent, their historical, scientific, or educational value, and may affect the eligibility of some sites for listing in the National Register of Historic Places.

Fair/Poor
: The diminished condition of selected archaeological resources has substantially reduced their historical, scientific, or educational value, and is likely to affect their eligibility for listing in the National Register of Historic Places.

Poor
: The degraded condition of known archaeological resources in general makes them ineffective in terms of historical, scientific, or educational value, and precludes their listing in the National Register of Historic Places.

Maritime Archaeological Resources Threat to Environment

16. **Do known maritime archaeological resources pose an environmental hazard and how is this threat changing?**

The sinking of a ship potentially introduces hazardous materials into the marine environment. This danger is true for historic shipwrecks as well. The issue is complicated by the fact that shipwrecks older than 50 years may be considered historical resources and must, by federal mandate, be protected. Many historic shipwrecks, particularly early to mid-20th century, still have the potential to retain oil and fuel in tanks and bunkers. As shipwrecks age and deteriorate, the potential for release of these materials into the environment increases.

Good
: Known maritime archaeological resources pose few or no environmental threats.

Good/Fair
: Selected maritime archaeological resources may pose isolated or limited environmental threats, but substantial or persistent impacts are not expected.

Fair
: Selected maritime archaeological resources may cause measurable, but not severe, impacts to certain sanctuary resources or areas, but recovery is possible.

Fair/Poor
: Selected maritime archaeological resources pose substantial threats to certain sanctuary resources or areas, and prospects for recovery are uncertain.

Poor
: Selected maritime archaeological resources pose serious threats to sanctuary resources, and recovery is unlikely.

Maritime Archaeological Resources Human Activities

17. What are the levels of human activities that may influence maritime archaeological resource quality and how are they changing?

Some human maritime activities threaten the physical integrity of submerged archaeological resources. Archaeological site integrity is compromised when elements are moved, removed, or otherwise damaged. Threats come from looting by divers, inadvertent damage by scuba diving visitors, improperly conducted archaeology that does not fully document site disturbance, anchoring, groundings, and commercial and recreational fishing activities, among others.

Good	Few or no activities occur that are likely to negatively affect maritime archaeological resource integrity.
Good/Fair	Some potentially relevant activities exist, but they do not appear to have had a negative effect on maritime archaeological resource integrity.
Fair	Selected activities have resulted in measurable impacts to maritime archaeological resources, but evidence suggests effects are localized, not widespread.
Fair/Poor	Selected activities have caused or are likely to cause severe impacts, and cases to date suggest a pervasive problem.
Poor	Selected activities warrant widespread concern and action, as large-scale, persistent, and/or repeated severe impacts have occurred or are likely to occur.

Appendix B:
Consultation with Experts and Document Review

The process for preparing condition reports (and similarly, this addendum) involves a combination of accepted techniques for collecting and interpreting information gathered from subject matter experts. The approach varies somewhat from sanctuary to sanctuary, in order to accommodate differing styles for working with partners. The Gray's Reef National Marine Sanctuary approach was closely related to the Delphi Method, a technique designed to organize group communication among a panel of geographically dispersed experts by using questionnaires, ultimately facilitating the formation of a group judgment. This method can be applied when it is necessary for decision-makers to combine the testimony of a group of experts, whether in the form of facts or informed opinion, or both, into a single useful statement.

The Delphi Method relies on repeated interactions with experts who respond to questions with a limited number of choices to arrive at the best supported answers. Feedback to the experts allows them to refine their views, gradually moving the group toward the most agreeable judgment. For condition reports, the Office of National Marine Sanctuaries uses 17 questions related to the status and trends of sanctuary resources, with accompanying descriptions and five possible choices that describe resource condition (Appendix A).

In order to address the 17 questions, sanctuary staff selected and consulted outside experts familiar with water quality, living resources, habitat, and maritime archaeological resources. A small workshop (21 participants) was convened in January 2012, where experts participated in facilitated discussions about each of the 17 questions. Experts represented various affiliations, including: Coastal Carolina University, Center for Marine and Wetlands Studies; Georgia Department of Natural Resources, Coastal Resources Division; Georgia Southern University, Applied Coastal Research Laboratory; Georgia Southern University, Department of Biology; Jacksonville University; NOAA Center for Coastal Environmental Health & Biomolecular Research; NOAA Center for Coastal Monitoring and Assessment; NOAA Fisheries Service, Fisheries Ecosystem Branch;

NOAA Fisheries Service, Southeast Regional Office; NOAA Gray's Reef National Marine Sanctuary; NOAA Office of National Marine Sanctuaries; Skidaway Institute of Oceanography; South Atlantic Fishery Management Council; South Carolina Department of Natural Resources, Marine Resources Research Institute, Offshore Finfish Section; University of Connecticut, Northeast Underwater Research Technology & Education Center; and University of Georgia, Center for Applied Isotope Studies.

At the workshop, each expert was introduced to the questions and then asked to provide recommendations and supporting arguments. The group supplemented the input with further discussion. In order to ensure consistency with Delphic methods during the discussion, a critical role of the facilitator was to minimize dominance of the discussion by a single individual or opinion (which often leads to "follow the leader" tendencies in group meetings) and to encourage the expression of honest differences of opinion. As discussions progressed, the group converged in their opinion of the rating that most accurately describes the current resource condition. After an appropriate amount of time, the facilitator asked whether the group could agree on a rating for the question, as defined by specific language linked to each rating (see Appendix A). If an agreement was reached, the result was recorded and the group moved on to consider the trend in the same manner. If agreement was not reached, the facilitator instructed sanctuary staff to consider all input and decide on a rating and trend at a future time, and to send their ratings back to workshop participants for individual comment.

Experts at the workshops were also given the opportunity to qualify their level of confidence in status and trend ratings by characterizing the sources of information they used to make judgments. A ranking of information quality was provided for three potential categories: data, literature, and personal experience. For each status or trend rating, the experts documented the source of information for each category. The confidence ratings, modified from Halpern et al. (2007), correlate with levels of information quality, as shown in the table below.

LEVEL OF CONFIDENCE				
1	2	3	4	5
HIGH UNCERTAINTY	SPECULATIVE	REASONABLE INFERENCE	MODERATE CERTAINTY	HIGH CERTAINTY
No data available, and no substantive personal experience	Few data and little information available, and limited personal experience	Some data available, unpublished or in non-peer reviewed sources, or some direct personal experience	Data available, some existing peer-reviewed publications, or direct personal experience	Considerable data available, extensive record of publication, or extensive personal experience or expertise

The scores compiled during the workshop were as follows:

QUESTION	STATUS RATING			TREND RATING		
	DATA	LITERATURE	PERSONAL EXPERIENCE	DATA	LITERATURE	PERSONAL EXPERIENCE
1	3	3	3	3	3	3
2						
3						
4						
5	4	4	4			
6	4	4	4			
7	4	4	4	4	4	4
8	3	3	3	3	3	3
9	4	4	4	4	4	4
10	4	4	4	3	3	3
11	3	3	3	3	3	3
12	3	3	3	3	3	3
13	2	2	2	2	2	2
14	2	2	2	2	2	2
15						
16						
17						

The first draft of the addendum summarized the opinions and uncertainty expressed by the experts, who based their input on knowledge and perceptions of local conditions. Comments and citations received from the experts were included, as appropriate, in text supporting the ratings.

The first draft of the addendum was sent to the workshop invitees (including those who attended and those who had been invited to the workshop but could not attend) for what was called an Initial Review, a four-week period that allowed them to ensure that the report accurately reflected their input, identify information gaps, provide comments or suggest revisions to the ratings and text. Upon receiving those comments, the writing team revised the text and ratings as they deemed appropriate.

In March 2012, a draft final report was sent to Dr. Jim Bohnsack (NOAA), Dr. Erv Garrison (University of Georgia), and Dr. Matthew Gilligan (Savannah State University) for final review. This External Peer Review is a requirement that started in December 2004, when the White House Office of Management and Budget (OMB) issued a Final Information Quality Bulletin for Peer Review (OMB Bulletin) establishing peer review standards that would enhance the quality and credibility of the federal government's scientific information. Along

with other information, these standards apply to Influential Scientific Information, which is information that can reasonably be determined to have a "clear and substantial impact on important public policies or private sector decisions." The Condition Reports are considered Influential Scientific Information. For this reason, these reports are subject to the review requirements of both the Information Quality Act and the OMB Bulletin guidelines. Therefore, following the completion of every condition report, they are reviewed by a minimum of three individuals who are considered to be experts in their field, were not involved in the development of the report, and are not ONMS employees. Comments from these peer reviews were incorporated into the final text of the report. Furthermore, OMB Bulletin guidelines require that reviewer comments, names, and affiliations be posted on the agency website, http://www.cio.noaa.gov. Reviewer comments, however, are not attributed to specific individuals. Comments by the External Peer Reviewers are posted at the same time as the formatted final document.

The reviewers were asked to review the technical merits of resource ratings and accompanying text, as well as to point out any omissions or factual errors. Following the External Peer Review, the comments and recommendations of the reviewers were considered by sanctuary staff and incorporated, as appropriate, into a final draft document. In some cases, sanctuary staff reevaluated the status and trend ratings and when appropriate, the accompanying text in the document was edited to reflect the new ratings. The final interpretation, ratings and text in the draft condition report were the responsibility of sanctuary staff, with final approval by the sanctuary superintendent. To emphasize this important point, authorship of the report is attributed to the sanctuary alone. Subject experts were not authors, though their efforts and affiliations are acknowledged in the report.

Acknowledgements

The staff of Gray's Reef National Marine Sanctuary would like to acknowledge the assistance and efforts of subject area experts who, by participating in a workshop in January 2012, provided responses to questions that guided the drafting of the "State of Sanctuary Resources" section of this addendum: Clark Alexander (Skidaway Institute of Oceanography and Georgia Southern University Applied Coastal Research Laboratory), Peter Auster (Sea Research Foundation – Mystic Aquarium and Department of Marine Sciences at the University of Connecticut), Myra Brouwer (South Atlantic Fishery Management Council), Marc Frischer (Skidaway Institute of Oceanography), Paul Gayes (Coastal Carolina University, Center for Marine and Wetlands Studies), Pat Geer (Georgia Department of Natural Resources, Coastal Resources Division), Danny Gleason (Georgia Southern University, Department of Biology), Nisse Goldberg (Jacksonville University), Jeff Hyland (NOAA Center for Coastal Environmental Health & Biomolecular Research), Todd Kellison (NOAA Fisheries Service, Fisheries Ecosystem Branch), Matt Kendall (NOAA Center for Coastal Monitoring and Assessment), Laura Kracker (NOAA Center for Coastal Environmental Health & Biomolecular Research), Jack McGovern (NOAA Fisheries Service, Southeast Regional Office), Scott Noakes (University of Georgia, Center for Applied Isotope Studies), and Marcel Reichert (South Carolina Department of Natural Resources, Marine Resources Research Institute, Offshore Finfish Section). Finally, our sincere thanks are extended to the peer reviewers of this document: Dr. Jim Bohnsack (NOAA NMFS), Dr. Erv Garrison (University of Georgia), and Dr. Matthew Gilligan (Savannah State University).

Notes

THE NATIONAL MARINE SANCTUARY SYSTEM

The Office of National Marine Sanctuaries, part of the National Oceanic and Atmospheric Administration, serves as the trustee for a system of 14 marine protected areas encompassing more than 150,000 square miles of ocean and Great Lakes waters. The 13 national marine sanctuaries and one marine national monument within the National Marine Sanctuary System represent areas of America's ocean and Great Lakes environment that are of special national significance. Within their waters, giant humpback whales breed and calve their young, coral colonies flourish, and shipwrecks tell stories of our maritime history. Habitats include beautiful coral reefs, lush kelp forests, whale migrations corridors, spectacular deep-sea canyons, and underwater archaeological sites. These special places also provide homes to thousands of unique or endangered species and are important to America's cultural heritage. Sites range in size from less than one to almost 140,000 square miles and serve as natural classrooms, cherished recreational spots, and are home to valuable commercial industries.

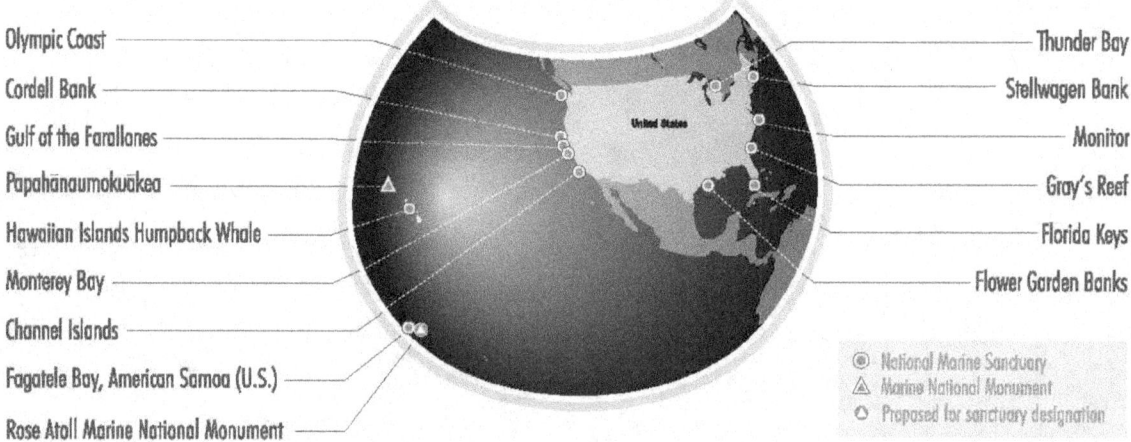

Olympic Coast

Cordell Bank

Gulf of the Farallones

Papahānaumokuākea

Hawaiian Islands Humpback Whale

Monterey Bay

Channel Islands

Fagatele Bay, American Samoa (U.S.)

Rose Atoll Marine National Monument

Thunder Bay

Stellwagen Bank

Monitor

Gray's Reef

Florida Keys

Flower Garden Banks

United States

◉ National Marine Sanctuary
△ Marine National Monument
○ Proposed for sanctuary designation

Scale varies in this perspective. Adapted from National Geographic Maps.

The Office of National
Marine Sanctuaries
is part of NOAA's
National Ocean Service.

VISION - People value marine sanctuaries as treasured places protected for future generations.

MISSION - To serve as the trustee for the nation's system of marine protected areas to conserve, protect and enhance their biodiversity, ecological integrity and cultural legacy.

NATIONAL MARINE
SANCTUARIES

www.ingramcontent.com/pod-product-compliance
Lightning Source LLC
Chambersburg PA
CBHW080348290526
45791CB00009BA/2791